MOUNTAIN MEMORIES III

by
J. Dennis Deitz

J. Dennis Deitz

With a Foreword by
David A. Bice

Jalamap Publications, Inc.,
833 Scenic Drive, Charleston, WV 25311
© 1984 J. Dennis Deitz
All rights reserved
Printed in The United States of America
ISBN 0-934750-59-9

Dedicated to our children
Joyce, Jaye and Linda Kay

Cover Page

The chimney stands stark and alone against a blue-gray mountain sky on a lonely West Virginia hilltop, a statue to a young pioneer couple who cleared a forest, built a house and cut the stone for this symbol of the pioneer spirit.

As they built it, little did they know that it would withstand 10,000 winds and winter storms and still be standing more than a century later - a personal monument to them.

It is a reminder of the house it served: the house that rang with the laughter of their children and their children's children and on and on for more than a dozen decades, as well as the hundreds of descendants of this pioneer couple.

Of all of the people who pass it today, is it only their descendants who get a warm feeling of home mixed with a sad nostalgic feeling for a way of life which may be gone forever?

It remains the only evidence left on the farm that this pioneer couple, John B. and Elizabeth Nutter, ever passed this way.

Table of Contents

Foreward vii
Introduction viii

FAMILY EARLY SETTLERS
   A Typical Early Settler 1
   My Grandfather's House 5
   Isaac Nutter 13
   My Grandfather's Farm 15
   Hunting 22
   Nutter Genealogy 25

FARM LIFE
   Making Maple Syrup And Sugar 31
   Death Of My Great-Grandfather's Maple Grove 35
   Working On Country Roads 37
   Apple Trees In Our Hills 40
   Raising And Shearing Sheep 43
   Hog Butchering 46
   Honey 49

MOUNTAIN TRUE STORIES
   Alexander David Deitz 52
   My Childhood Friend And Hero 56
   The Rupert Bank 58
   The Murder Of Zona Heaster 66
   The Unlawful Baptism Of Edward Shue 68
   Mediums 71
   An Addition About My Father 73

MY FATHER AND BROTHER
   Watson Deitz And new Prospect School 78
   Something About Granville A. Deitz 85
   Fletcher And Granville 87
   A Story About Granville Deitz 90
   Our Neighbor 93
   A Mountain Debate Of About 1914 96
   Was It A Rat, Or Was It A Mouse? 101
   The Letter Writer 103

Vital Statistics 106
West Virginia Horse Traders 108
Pay Day In Pax 110

MY MOTHER'S STORIES
Memories 114
By Betty Nutter Deitz 118
My Little Big Dennis 127
My Dear Little Pearl 130
Greed 132
The Intelligence Of Animals .134
Small Narrations Of Dogs And
Their Intelligence 136
Children's Tracks 141
Legs For The Chiefty 145
Poems 147

SPOOFS
Morel Madness 164
Mountaineer Mania, Or
What About Them 'Eers? 169
How To Recognize Mountaineer Mania 174
The Carbide Retirees Bridge Club 176
Archie and The Diesel Cadillac 179

FOREWORD

Recollections, memories, and remembrances are as Shakespeare said, "the warder of the brain." Dennis Deitz makes no pretenses about his writings being Shakespearian quality, but he does serve us as a warder or guardian of the past. His stories of growing up on a farm in the early 1900's stir the fondest memories for many of us and for others allow a glimpse into a lifetime we were unfortunate not to have experienced.

Mountain Memories III continues to permit the reader to vicariously experience the life of Mr. Deitz through the written word. This series of books will probably never hit the *New York Times* reviews or best seller lists but will have more impact and give more enjoyment to readers than ninety-five percent of the books which do. Historians in the future will look to the works of writers of Mr. Deitz's perception much more than those who pass through an area "looking for a story." Dennis Deitz is the story.

David A. Bice

INTRODUCTION

In *Mountain Memories II,* I told of my people: my deceased brother, Granville, my parents, my grandparents and other people I have known. Mostly, though, I wanted to picture mountain farm life as I know it.

It seemed strange to me the interest shown by readers who never knew any of my people, or even did not know me, in my family stories. I have received many letters and have been told this by numerous people. Many interesting incidents have been recited about their people by these correspondents.

It sometimes seems that *Mountain Memories I* and *Mountain Memories II* get credit for the recollections about other people's lives, and the story teller will say that this is the first time these incidents have been recalled in forty or fifty years. Many times someone calls or writes and will use almost the same words, saying, "These books are almost like a visit through my childhood," or "I read these books again and relive my childhood."

Maybe this confirms my belief that more interesting, funny things happen in every day life than anyone can make up or invent in the way of stories.

In *Mountain Memories III* are some additional stories about my family. These stories have been given to me by people who went to school to my parents or worked with my brother, Granville. Also included are some writings by my mother. Mainly though, I have carried my family back one more generation, to my Great-Grandfather, John B. Nutter, and his wife, Elizabeth (Pitsenbarger), who settled and made a farm from a vast virgin forest. The farm where I grew up was part of their farm. I have tried to describe their lives and struggles from what I have been told by their children who were a part of pioneer West Virginia. Maybe they were of the last West Virginia pioneers.

The methods and tools they used, as well as their schools and churches, were in a small way a part of my early life on a farm, and I have tried to describe this life.

I want to thank and give credit to the people mentioned in this book who contributed stories about my people. I especially want to thank Kathleen Hensley Browning for her invaluable help with editing and typing. I am indebted greatly to my wife, Madeline, whose judgment I seldom questioned as to what was worthwhile.

Dennis Deitz

A Typical Early Settler

My great-grandfather was typical of the settlers who explored and conquered the wilderness of America. He was in the forefront of the vast migration of pioneers who cleared the forests and turned the first sod to farm the virgin land. He was only one of the thousands who did the same type of pioneering.

John and Elizabeth Nutter came to the Hickory Flats country because John B. was able to purchase uncleared land in that area. There were few nearby neighbors, but Elizabeth's parents lived about two miles away, and his two brothers settled south of him. Her uncle, John Miller Amick, had settled on Anglins' Creek about two miles away, thirty years before. There is a written account of this uncle and aunt coming from Pendleton County on horseback all the way by blazed trails to Elizabeth's parents' home.

With them were their two children and their belongings. Three miles before reaching their destination they crossed a clear mountain stream, or "crick," as they called it. Here they rested, along with their horses, before going up the long mountain trail. The young wife and mother took off her shoes and waded in the cool stream. She then announced to her husband, "Old man, here is where we will build our home." That was where they did make their home, raising fourteen children. I have the story of these settlers and their descendants. The fourteen children were first cousins to John B.'s wife, Elizabeth, my great-grandmother. The book has helped me to learn the details of the early settlers' daily life and work.

John B. and Elizabeth were settlers thirty years later, yet conditions still remained the same. They were almost the last generation to settle in a vast virgin, uncleared forest in West Virginia, and all their lives they did back-breaking, hard labor. Never again in the state, or maybe in the Appalachian Mountains, did a young couple face the same challenges, and see the sights they saw in the untamed mountains with few neighbors and only horse trails connecting them in this wild majestic range.

The more I learn about these pioneers, the more I am amazed at the abilities they had and used to survive and prosper in the wilderness. They were almost masters of all crafts needed on a farm. They could do carpentry work, make their own furniture, and build a log cabin and barn. They were their own blacksmiths, great woodsmen and hunters. Many of them were knowledgeable about the soil and farming, and they doctored their own animals.

Many of their wives knew and raised their own herbs, which they gathered to doctor their own families. They delivered babies, wove their wool and flax to make lindsey woolsey cloth, and wove wool for cloth for clothes, bedclothes, socks and mittens. The wool came from the sheep they raised, and the flax was grown on the farm.

These people weren't just jack-of-all-trades, but were more like masters of all trades.

I am overwhelmed at the thought that if I had been born 75 to 100 years earlier I would have had to face these pioneer conditions.

John B. Nutter came to Hickory Flats in the fall of 1851, living in a lean-to open-faced building in the hollow below where my "grandfather's house" stood. During that winter he cleared land for farming and built a log house, probably trading labor with two brothers who did the same thing in nearby wind-protected hollows, or, as they would have called them, "hollers."

From the hilltops, John Nutter could see miles of virgin forests, which were mostly hardwoods, and the valleys were full of evergreens, which were mostly hemlock in our country.

The roads were trails or paths, sometimes called trace paths, just wide enough for travel by horseback.

In the spring he brought his young wife and two young sons, Alfred and Andrew Scott, to their new home. With one cow and two horses they started their life of farming.

The first crop planted by the pioneers was usually corn, which was needed for bread. The corn for bread was probably ground at Elizabeth's Uncle John Miller Amick's grist mill on Anglins' Creek two miles away. The corn was also needed to feed the cow and two horses. They would have had a garden in the summer of 1852, and there would have been wild blackberries and grapes. Chestnuts would help for food in the fall and early winter, and hickory nuts and walnuts would last through most of the winter. The early spring would bring wild greens and wild strawberries on newly cleared "new ground." I am sure they obtained apples and other fruit from the farm of Elizabeth's parents, Peter and Elizabeth Pitzenbarger, about two miles away, where they had settled about 40 years before.

The north end of his property started at Sugar Grove Knob, where the Sugar Grove fire tower now stands. John and Elizabeth built their cabin about a mile below this point.

How Great-grandfather accomplished so much in such a short period of time is not clear, for his sons would have been too young to help, but he may have traded small sections of his large holdings for labor.

He must have gotten the start for his orchards from his father-in-law, and he may have gotten his start in farm animals from the same source by either buying, trading or even borrowing them. At any rate, he was supposed to have had a lot of farm stock within a short time.

John B. could have been capable of splitting his own rails and building his own snake rail fence in the winter as he was supposed to have been a big, strong man and an expert with an axe, as well as with wedges, sledgehammers, wooden mauls and gluts (wooden wedges), the tools needed to split rails. He also owned chestnut trees, which were almost beyond value to the survival of the pioneers. The chestnut logs split easily to make rails and were used to build log cabins, shingles for the roofs and even furniture. The chestnuts were used for food for the families and fattened the hogs which were turned loose in the woods to root for the nuts. The hogs were butchered after cold weather came in late fall.

John B. built a tanning vat where he tanned leather for himself and neighbors. He may have traded leather for labor or sold the leather for needed cash.

He must have been fairly prosperous by the late 1850's as he was able to build the large house on the flat mountain top, the house I call "my grandfather's house." This house was built with sawed lumber, so he must have been fairly prosperous to have had money for sawed lumber and nails. He may have been able to cut his own logs and take them to a water powered sawmill, or he may have gotten them sawed by giving the sawmill owner a part of the lumber or logs. This house stood for 125 years until 1980, when it burned.

According to family tradition, he had accumulated a fair amount of cash in the form of gold by the time of the Civil War and was supposed to have kept it hidden in the grain bins, from the marauding Civil War soldiers and renegades.

He was able to hire a lot of farm labor, and he gave his children farms before his death from pneumonia in 1893.

Did Great-grandfather John see the sky almost darkened with the migration flights of the passenger pigeons? I don't know, but I do know that Great-grandfather Deitz saw this some twenty years earlier from a farm about five miles away. Millions of passenger pigeons used the areas as a roost on their migration flights, and they would roost in such great numbers as to break limbs on trees. Maybe their flight pattern did not cross Hickory Flats, or maybe their numbers had been reduced by this time by the meat hunters in the North. Maybe they no longer made the migrations from their summer home in the north to their vacation homes in the south.

Elizabeth Nutter
Died in 1894 at 62 years.

John B. Nutter

My Grandfather's House

All my life when I have seen an old, abandoned farm house I have wondered about the people who had lived, loved and sorrowed there. This was especially true when I hunted or fished in what was strange country to me, maybe back in the hills of Pocahontas County. I might be on a lonely mountain top on a long abandoned farm and come to an old farm house falling down. It might have once been a beautiful house with a lovely view.

With a lot of time to hunt and enjoy the beautiful scenes, I would always start imagining or wondering about the people who lived there, maybe as far back as one hundred years before. Who were they? Had they loved their remote lovely mountain home, their farm life, their view?

What were the stories of the people who lived there? Did many of them live and die there? Did they have great joys and deep sorrows? Wouldn't it be great if the house which held these stories could communicate them? When and where had the children, grandchildren, and maybe great-grandchildren gone? What were their legends?

Since I don't know the stories of these places, I will tell you about the West Virginia mountain farm in Nicholas and Greenbrier Counties that I do know about: the story of my Grandfather Isaac Nutter's house and the children who grew to adulthood there and their children. Actually only one generation of children was born and grew up there, and my Grandfather Nutter was one of those children. He was born there in 1856 and died there in 1935. He actually raised his own children on the adjoining farm, where I was born, and then moved back into the old house after his own children were grown and married. Later in this chapter a list of Grandfather's brothers, and sisters will be given, with a list of most of their descendants for one to three generations, as well as where they settled.

Great-grandfather John Nutter and his wife, Elizabeth (Pitzenbarger) Nutter came to this farm early in their married life with two small sons from a farm near or now under the waters of the Summersville Dam in Nicholas County. This farm-to-be was uncleared land about 1851, and Great-grandfather John Nutter spent the winter in the hollow below where the house later stood, living in a lean-to while he built a cabin for the family and cleared the land for planting. His two brothers did the same thing in adjoining hollows.

John Nutter prospered here in his new log cabin. He built vats for tanning leather, cleared land for farming, and bred, raised, traded and sold farm animals. Here my Grandfather Isaac was born in 1856. About this time his father started the big house on top of a flat hill top, a part of Hickory Flats, the house I call my grandfather's house. It was about thirty-six by forty-five feet, but was not a log house. It had milled lumber throughout, including the siding. The nails seem to have been hand-made or cast. Since grandfather's house burned in 1980, after one hundred twenty-five years, these nails can still be found in the ashes.

It was a long, low house, and the upper story was one long room about twenty by forty-five feet. It was often used to store great bins of threshed oats and wheat. I remember that my grandfather also did this at times. Since they had granaries, I suppose this was done to protect the grain from rats and mice as they had several cats which stayed around the house and kept the rodents depopulated. Legend has it that John Nutter kept gold in the bins of loose grain to keep it hid from the marauding soldiers of both the North and South during the Civil War.

John Nutter was supposed to have been fairly prosperous by this time and had several farm "hands" employed at times during the planting, cultivating and harvesting of the crops. He saved a large grove of maple trees, and a year's supply of maple sugar was made each winter and spring from the sap collected from the maple trees.

A few years later after the house was built, John Nutter built a large barn. The inside frame was made of huge poplar logs, about three feet wide and ten inches thick. A log rolling day was set after all of the logs had been cut and grooved to fit, with each log scheduled to go in a certain place. The frame of the inside of the barn was probably forty-five feet long and twenty-five feet deep. There was a driveway through the center for teams and wagons. This was perhaps twenty-five feet high. I am not sure how the logs were lifted twenty to twenty-five feet, and in later years when I asked people this question, they could only speculate. It was thought they had poles as thick as telephone poles placed at an angle, one end on the ground and the other end on top of the last placed top log, and the notched log slid up the slanted poles. It is possible that teams of horses were used to pull them to the top with the use of log chains, or pulleys might have been used. The legend was that this was accomplished in only one or two days.

After this, sheds were built about fifteen feet beyond this sixty-five by fifty foot log framing, all the way around this inner log structure. A double wooden shingle roof covered all of this. This was a showplace barn in size in our country, although not as large as the huge barns built on much larger farms west of our state and in Pennsylvania.

This barn stood for almost 100 years before the outside structure fell while its ownership was outside the family. Some of the log structure still stands. The wooden pegs used in anchoring the logs together could still be seen a few years ago.

I was involved in many games of hide and seek in the hay mows in this barn on rainy days when I was a child.

There were many other outbuildings around the house, including the outhouse. One of the rooms in the granary held a barrel of gasoline, for my grandfather owned a car as far back as I can remember, and there were just a few gas pumps in front of country stores for miles around. There was a large woodshed back of the house where a supply of wood for the winter was stored for the fireplace and the kitchen stove. A building to remember was the spring house where the fresh milk and butter were kept. This was a small building made of huge, cut stones up to about four feet. Above the stones were logs going up another four feet, and there was a floor between the cellar room and the roof top. The floor of the spring house was of natural stone already there, but leveled and smoothed with tools. A place was chiseled out of the stone bottom about a foot wide, five feet long, and a couple of inches lower than the rest of the stone floor. Cold spring water flowed through this, and crocks of milk and butter with lids were set there to be kept cool. Other perishable foods were placed there also. This was our refrigeration.

I can imagine that the amount of good food that passed through this spring house and into the stomachs of the descendants of John B. and Elizabeth Nutter could only be counted by the ton, and maybe the amount of cholesterol by the peck!

I still have wonderful memories of my Grandfather's house and farm. They had moved back to the home place before I was born, so they always lived there in my memory. The front porch, which was inset or recessed, was about twenty feet wide and fifteen feet deep. At one time it was enclosed across the front, but I only know this because of a picture which was taken when Aunt Rosa and Uncle Marvin lived there. There was a porch swing and probably some type of couch. I remember Grandfather sitting there with a fly swatter and killing flies. He would make marks on the porch floor where the sunshine and shade met at certain hours, and the next day he would check the change at the same hour.

He liked to challenge my sister, who was two years older than I, to climb up the inside of the door facing. She could do this easily by placing her hands and feet flat against the facing and pressing her hands and feet hard against the opposite facing, climbing all the way to the top. This must have been at noon or Sunday as most of the time he was a hard working surveyor and farmer and didn't sit on the porch much.

Our house was on the west of our knob field, on a bench well below the top of the hill, and his house and barn were on a big, level field on top of the hill. From his house the sunrise could be seen through a gap in the ridge east of his farm. The sunrise through the gap in the next mountain was beautiful, first peeping through the trees and then coming into full view, with mists or fog lying in the valley between the hills. Sometimes these fogs were more like clouds, thick and white. Other times the fogs only covered the tops of the ridges.

The front porch was shaded, and we sat there for a noon day break after we had eaten. Someone blew on an old cow horn as a signal for us to come to eat. This horn was from a cow which had mooed her last moo in the long distant past, and this horn was her only monument left from her life.

His house was large with low ceilings, and it was usually cool in the summer heat. There was a large living room, three bedrooms, a kitchen, dining room, utility room and a hall. Back of the hallway, underneath the steps, was a storage room for apples to be stored in the winter. With rooms all around it, apples would never freeze there. There was also a huge room upstairs. A wonderful odor penetrated the whole house from these stored apples.

The spring house helped to satisfy my appetite, for it was full of crocks of milk sitting in the cold water, and it was always cool there. I was always free to go there to get as much butter or milk to go with bread and honey or homemade jellies and jams as I wanted. These were far superior to anything found today.

What I remember best was listening to the story tellers at Grandfather's house, or maybe at our house. When a few of them gathered together and started recalling incidents from the past, we children sat and listened, absolutely fascinated. They might be telling stories we had heard many times, but that didn't matter. We would listen open-mouthed to the stories as they were repeated. Some of these story tellers might be illiterate, but could they use words! They could paint a picture with words and gestures. The same story told by another story teller might sound different because each one had his own individual way of story telling, and the words and descriptions might result in a different version of the story. We made many excuses to get to listen to these story tellers. Certain ones were special, and we felt we just had to listen to their stories.

A history and genealogy of the children who were born or grew up in Grandfather's house will follow. They are the children of John B. Nutter, born in 1826, and Elizabeth (Pitsenbarger) Nutter, born in 1830. Many of their grandchildren are still living in 1984. Even more interesting is that some of the great-grandchildren of David Nutter (John B.'s father), born in 1769, are still living 214 years later. There is one case of four generations being born in just 46 years.

The Wives Of
Grandfather's House

There were only two wives who ever lived in Grandfather's house for any length of time: my grandmother and my great-grandmother. My great-grandmother died many years before I was born, but, as far as I know, she was the only woman who gave birth to and raised a family in the house. She was Elizabeh (Pitsenbarger) Nutter, wife of John B. Nutter. Her mother was Elizabeth (Amick) Pitzenbarger, who was of Dutch ancestry, and was remembered as having a heavy Dutch accent. This accent was supposed to have been the source of many great stories which were being repeated nearly 100 years later by her nieces and nephews, and on through her great nieces and great nephews. These stories were not repeated by her direct descendants, and I suppose the reason I never heard the stories was that her own children were used to mixed English and Dutch, knew what she meant, and didn't notice it as being funny, as it was to others.

One of her great nieces told me of the stories recently, but because of her great age she could only remember that there were stories, but she could not remember details. The great niece told me that Elizabeth Nutter was greatly loved by these relatives, who enjoyed the hilarious statements she would come up with in her mixture of Dutch and English.

This relative said that most of her life she could repeat the stories, and even in her old age her grandchildren would visit and ask her to tell them stories about "Aunt Besty." The only story she could tell me was about the time a stranger, who was a cattle buyer, stopped by and asked her to see the Lord. Not having heard that term used to describe her husband, she thought he meant the bull, as the bull was nicknamed "The Lord" by the children, for he lorded over the other farm animals. She answered him by saying that the last time she saw him they were driving him around the fence to lock him in the barn. Later in the day the buyer had made his way off Hickory Flats to Meadow River at Russellville, where he saw her husband at his brother's place. Since he hadn't met her husband, he started telling him of the strange conversation which had taken place back on the mountain. Great-grandfather John immediately added two and two and knew who the man was speaking of. He was really embarrassed.

I remember my grandmother, Mary (Walker) Nutter, all of my life with fondness. She was quite different from Grandfather as she was serious, but very kind, whereas he had a great sense of humor. Her father had died when she was very young, and her mother had raised eight children all alone. Since she was one of the older children, she had to work hard and got very little education. By the time I knew my Grandmother, they were prosperous, and she had become very genteel and was always well dressed and looked neat. By this time they were able to travel, and she always had help with the house work. One lady and her son lived with them many years. Grandmother Nutter still loved to work in her garden, and her chickens were the love of her life. She had her own riding horse, "Old Buck," who lived about twenty-five years and was used for nothing else but for her to ride. Any time she wanted to go some place she would have someone saddle the horse, and she would mount him from a small platform called a stile. Off she would go, riding side-saddle.

She was also a midwife and delivered many children. I know she delivered me, and I always wanted to ask her if she regretted having delivered me. If I had asked her, she would have given me a serious answer.

My Great-great-grandmother, Christina O'Dell Nutter may have lived in the house for a time. She survived her husband, David Nutter, by about forty years. He was much older than she, and she lived to be over 100 years, as did my mother, her great-granddaughter. They knew each other and between them lived through the terms of all of the presidents of the United States except for President Reagan. My impression is that she lived most of the time with a younger son. She is listed in the 1860 census as a midwife.

Visitors At
Grandfather's House

As far as I was concerned, some of the people who came to visit in Grandfather's house were from far away places, but those places would not be a long drive now. The ones who made the longest trip to come for a visit were Grandfather's sister, Mahulda, and her husband Charles Amick. They were married in 1885 and soon after that homesteaded in South Dakota, where they proved up on 640 acres, or one square mile. They had a large family. They seemed to have a stop and go type of prosperity for sometimes the droughts wiped out their crops, or the crops might be good and the markets would be low, so they wouldn't prosper too well. Then they might have the entire 640 acres do well in a year when other areas were wiped out with droughts or blights. Then the market prices would be high, and their prosperity would carry them for three or four bad years.

They would usually visit in August between the harvest of the wheat and corn crops. Even on visits, except for Grandfather taking them to visit old friends, they were always helping with the work. I never knew then that her name was Mahulda. It was always Uncle Charley and Aunt Hulda. Aunt Hulda was always busy sewing, knitting or working in the kitchen. If idle time is the devil's time, Aunt Hulda never gave him one minute.

I remember Uncle Charley being quite different. He had moved out west when he was young, and his neighbors were different in thoughts and ideas from our people, and so was his reading material, if he read. My Grandfather was well read and traveled in his work, and he loved to tease Uncle Charley when he made a statement or offered an idea which was foreign to Grandfather.

I remember one statement made by Uncle Charley which was really funny to us. He was talking about one of Grandfather's and Aunt Hulda's nephews who had gone out west to work for Uncle Charley for several years. Uncle Charley said, "You know, he is a good worker, but he is always trying to invent something. That fool boy don't know that everything has already been invented."

That fool boy also had his own unique ideas. He came back east during the depression, got married and went to work in the mines. In 1952 Eisenhower, a Republican, was elected President. The next day he quit the mines, telling everyone that a person couldn't make a living under a Republican, so he was quitting. As far as I know, he never worked another day in his life.

There were other visitors I remember too. Both my grandparents and parents had partially helped raise several nieces and nephews who had lost one or both parents when young. Some of the relatives married someone who worked for the railroads or worked for the railroads themselves. They actually had vacations, something we (children) who lived on the farm had never heard of. We had fun when they came with their children for a visit. If I have sounded as if we worked all the time, that wasn't the whole story. These visits were during the slack season between crops. The visiting children would help with the chores and work, and my parents would give us play time. We would play on rainy days, especially Hide and Seek in Grandfather's barn. I couldn't believe how much these children loved to roam the fields and woods. To me, they were leading the glamorous life in town, with all kinds of free time. The day they left was sad and lonesome, especially their last vacation visits, for I think I realized I might never see them again, which proved to be the case with several of them. I played football against one of these boys in high school but didn't know who he was until he looked me up in the locker room after the game. We have both lived in the Kanawha Valley almost ever since and have never seen each other, although we call each other once in a while. When I have met some of the others through the years it seems sad and gives me a feeling of lonesomeness because I am not able to bring back the feeling of closeness and friendship we once had. Our first cousins seemed to be almost as close to us as most brothers and sisters are today.

ANDREW S. NUTTER FAMILY: front row - Etta holding Garnet, Verna, Andrew S. holding Ditha. Back row -Alden, Delbert. Andrew son of John and Elizabeth Nutter.

Isaac Nutter

In *Mountain Memories II* I wrote of my Grandfather, Isaac C. (Ike) Nutter. In it I told of working with him and how he was almost always teaching as we worked. I was never able to remember too many actual lessons or incidents. I had worked with him from the time I was very young, and the lessons and teachings were an on-going experience, with one lesson not standing out from another, but there was just an accumulation of learning and never questioning. I never had any reason to believe other than that he was right about what he told me.

When a cousin of mine, Frank Nutter, read *Mountain Memories II* he told me that he could remember a few exact lessons our Grandfather taught him. My cousin's experience with Grandfather was a little different in that he lived a few miles away and only began to help him when my cousin was a teenager and was more apt to question the reasons why things were done a certain way.

One incident he recalled was when he helped Grandfather load a wagon full of loose potatoes. Riding the the wagon seat, they drove several miles to market to sell them. Frank said when they had driven several miles that he turned and looked at the potatoes and said, "Granddad, all of the big potatoes have worked their way to the top." Grandfather said, "No, Frank, you are wrong. The big potatoes haven't worked their way to the top. The little potatoes have worked their way to the bottom." He then said, "Frank, let that be a lesson of life to you. The big people don't work their way to the top, the little people work their way to the bottom. Sometimes you will see two men start with the same type of farm and prospects. One will work long hours, expend a lot of energy and sweat, use his knowledge, rotate his crops and prosper. He hasn't worked his way to the top over anyone.

The other man just works enough to get by, doesn't try to rotate crops or clear new ground. In the end he has just worked his way to the bottom."

Another time when Frank was helping, Grandfather decided

he needed to make a new wagon tongue by cutting a small hickory tree to use for this purpose. They went to a forested area and up a hill to a point on the ridge where Grandfather found a long, straight hickory which was suitable for the wagon tongue. Frank then asked why they had come past all those hickory trees in the valley, for they wouldn't have to be dragged a great distance.

Grandfather told him, "Frank, the strongest, toughest, more flexible trees grow on the highest, windy points where the winds blow the hardest. Trees are just like people. The ones who have withstood and survived the roughest conditions are the ones who end up the strongest and toughest. Always remember that when conditions in life look the darkest." Frank said he had never forgotten this great advice through his lifetime, which included the great depression.

Although Grandfather aided and helped many people in need, he had little patience with people who wouldn't try or who wouldn't work. He said he wouldn't try to upstage God by trying to help those who wouldn't help themselves.

Granddad Nutter once pointed out a passing man and remarked, "There goes Brown. You know, he is an ignorant man but he doesn't know he's ignorant. That makes him dangerous. Now, you take Ed Hayes. He's ignorant and knows he's ignorant; therefore, he's a safe person.

Once Granddad was driving along a narrow country road in the ruts in the road when he saw Brown riding toward him on a horse on the edge of the road about a quarter mile away. Brown pulled to the center of the road, riding directly toward Granddad. Granddad remarked, "Do you see Brown? He is saying to himself, 'A man's entitled to half the road, and, by gad, I'm taking my half!'" So Granddad kept driving the ruts ahead until Brown had to wheel his horse to the side of the road. Brown yelled, "By gad, a man's entitled to half the road." — Granddad's exact words. Granddad just yelled back at him, "By golly, I'm taking my half."

Granddad was driving along through the ruts on one of the muddy roads with my brother when he suddenly pulled out of the ruts with the wheels riding the high places where it was rougher and jolted more. My brother asked, "Why don't you drive in the ruts where it is smoother riding?" Granddad replied, "A man should not spend his lifetime traveling in another man's ruts." He had just been setting my brother up for his reply.

I can just hear my Grandfather's answer to a modern day liberal politician who preaches that a hard working man owes a big healthy, worthless man a living while this same politician protects himself from paying increased taxes by voting himself increased wages and benefits.

Dennis Deitz

My Grandfather's Farm

In the woods around Grandfather's farm you could hear the songs of the birds and the sound of chipmunks rustling in the leaves, making me think that they were squirrels. I would have a glimpse of a squirrel peeping around the trunk of a tree, then quickly hiding behind the trunk and making its way to a thicket of leaves while I tried slowly and quietly to maneuver to a better vantage point to see it. The whole woods would seem to be waking up, the sun rising higher, shining in the top of the colorful trees, making a picture that lodged in my mind, for the timber would be a fairyland of color. The maples would be as red as fire, some of the oaks turned the color of red wine, and sourwood a rich red. The red oaks would be orange, and the poplars turned from green to shades of yellow and gold. The dogwoods had dull red leaves and clusters of red berries. The bright, brown full chestnuts would be falling on the forest floor where the chipmunks, squirrels, ferrie diddles and even the domestic hogs fattened up until they wobbled they were so fat. The squirrels would be busy storing the nuts for a long, cold winter in their little home-made cellars, as well as planting trees for the future.

The sun might set blood-red each day through the milky blue haze in the evening, but we knew that red skies at night usually meant fair weather tomorrow. The flaming red sumac leaves might match the gorgeous sunset, making a vivid contrast to the few evergreen trees which somehow had escaped the forest massacre of previous years.

One of the many things people watched in making their weather predictions was animal reaction, both domestic and wild. They would seem to be getting ready for a storm by either scurrying about gathering food or making beds.

There were many signs people noted which were thought to indicate a cold winter or a dry summer, but I don't remember many of them. I still don't have much faith in weather predictions by the weather men (now called meterologists) with their satelites and radar, and I wonder if they would be just as well off if they observed the many clues our forefathers did about what nature was telling them, as my Grandfather and his neighbors did. I am still convinced they were better forecasters than the weather forecasters of today, and especially the New England fishermen whose lives depended on forecasting storms. I have often read that these fishermen might look at the sky and suddenly say, "Let's head home. There's a storm coming," while a novice fisherman would look at the sky and not see anything different than the day before when they had fished until evening. Many times the man making the forecast couldn't explain how he knew this — he just knew. I believe it was a slight change in the look of the sky, a slight change in temperature and a slight change in air pressure, making the air feel different. Grandfather and others seemed to know these things, for many of their crops depended on not getting wet and rotfing in the fields. Therefore, they might work until dark to put the hay, wheat or oats into shocks.

They relied on the old saying, "Red skies in the morning, sailors take warning; red skies at night, sailors delight."

One weather prediction was that if it rained, cleared up, rained and cleared up again, that meant that if the clearing was in the north sky it would stay clear. If clouds dropped behind a semi-cloudy, hazy, low sky rain would come back. A prediction that came down from the Indians was, "If bad weather clear at night it not clear at all."

Once a hired lady who was at my brother's house when the first thunder was heard in the spring remarked, "If the first thunder in spring brings rain, it will be a rainy year." A rain followed, but only on one side of the house and farm. My brother asked her, "Does that mean we will have a rainy season on half the farm and a drought on the other side?"

My favorite weather prophet was a neighbor we boys always asked about the weather. If it were raining we would ask, "Do you think it will clear up?" And he would answer, "It always has." If we asked him if it were going to rain, he would answer, "It always has." I never knew him to be wrong in his predictions.

One of the things that has changed greatly in my lifetime has been the respect shown for our elders. This was taught to us as part of good manners, but there was more to it than that. Our elders had our respect because they earned respect. Grandfather was better educated than most of our neighbors and was better read than some, but, more than that, he was an observer and analyzed the things he saw. This was also true of many of our neighbors who were not as well educated as Grandfather. I was often astonished by the things they knew and their ability to improvise when a problem arose. Their economic lives depended on being able to resolve unexpected hardships, and a new tool or method might be originated.

Recently a man in his eighties, an ex-farmer, asked me about something I had written about Grandfather Deitz's cow which had walked across some boards which had been laid from the hills to the hay mow so hay could be put in the mow. The cow's legs had slipped between the boards. He wanted to know how the cow had been rescued, but I have never heard and don't know, but I can surmise as to how the problem was solved. Flat boards could have been secured or nailed close to her hind legs, and her lighter hind quarters might have been lifted with a wide leather strap so as to place more boards under her hind legs. Then, placing more boards in front of her, they might have been able to lift and, with the cow's help, get her to her feet and lead her out over the boards. Also, they might have had the help of a pulley. I have seen many things done on the farm that looked to be impossible to do.

My people and the neighbors earned respect because of their knowledge of the soil. I once read about Jesse Stuart who told of his people picking up a handful of soil and actually tasting it and then saying what would grow there. I never saw this done by my people, but I have a theory about it. I presume they were tasting it for acidity, knowing that certain crops would not grow in soil high in acid, but something else would. Now the soil can be tested by County Agricultural Agents, who can tell exactly which mineral is missing.

Our people did not move to a farm they were not acquainted with, for Grandfather's family had farmed the same land for 75 years and knew which fields grew which crops the best, and they knew about crop rotation. Yet I have seen farmers pick up soil and test it by feel and sight, for they could tell if it had enough clay to hold moisture and enough loam to be loose enough to allow the roots to spread.

Some of our people were slow to change when the County Agents came with their bulletins and suggestions, and they might say, "The way my father did things is good enough for me." Others might be conservative and slow to change until more proof was given, but Grandfather was well read and liked to try new things, some of which were totally wrong for our area. Naturally new ideas about farming, forests and streams were questioned until they were proved to be right.

I remember one new idea which proved to be a disaster: the multiflora rose, which could be planted in rows to form natural fences for stock so there would be no more expensive fence building. The County Agents really carried the message and sold many farmers on the idea, but they didn't talk to the birds. The careless birds ate the seed pods and didn't plant the seed in the straight fence rows as they should have in order to help the farmers. As a result, the roses came up all over the fields, and the farmers have been trying to eradicate them ever since.

That raises a question: when is an expert an expert? Had the "expert" really observed as being practical what he recommended to the farmers, or had he been proclaimed an expert by someone who was "gung-ho" about a new idea? Or had he been designated to be an expert by someone who had the same point of view?

I think the big difference from the days I remember on Grandfather's farm and today is that we saw more in nature and enjoyed things we saw and heard, for we didn't have the distractions which are so abundant today. We didn't just gulp life down without tasting, hearing, smelling and seeing things around us. We heard the sounds of animals and birds in the woods, enjoyed the sight of mixed sun and shaded spots on the country roads, and loved the smell of the sun-lit woods, trees and flowers.

As I walked the country roads, in the fog sometimes, I seemed to be walking through an eerie, ghost-like world, almost in total silence, free of sounds from the birds and animals until the sun burned the fog from the hills.

As I grew older I helped Grandfather with all kinds of farm work when I could be spared from the same type of work on our farm. The main difference was that he had a huge barn, and all of his hay would be stored in the hay mows. It was my job to tramp the hay into the mows to pack it down and make more room. That was a hot, dusty job, tramping it against the roof of the barn!

I think the thing that made our longer, harder hours so much more enjoyable was that we always could get a sense of accomplishment from it, for we could see the results immediately. On the farm we could see things grow, ripen and be reaped, cut or gathered and then eaten or sold for cash, which was scarce.

I think yet today the reason people like to have a garden is that they like to watch things grow and to get their hands in the soil. It is, no doubt, part of our nature and our heritage. As an old mountain woman said to her hard working husband who hated to lose a minute's work, "You work like every day is a race with the sunset."

My first job for Grandfather was probably to "fetch and carry." When I was fairly young he used to call for me to catch his work horses in the large hillside field. I could always go out in the field, without bridle or saddle, and catch the horses. I would ride one horse bareback to the barn, and the other one would follow. Those horses just wouldn't let him catch them, and I used to tell him that the horses didn't trust everyone. Sometimes he gave me some salty replies, but he was rather tolerant about jokes.

When I was young it was my job to carry drinking water for

the harvest "hands" when they were working under the hot sun cradling oats and wheat. They drank and sweated water by the bucket full! We had some buckets which had held five pounds of lard and probably held a half gallon of water, and I have watched men drink all the water from one of these buckets without removing the bucket from their mouths.

Later I graduated to heavier chores, maybe with some reluctance, but it helped my ego to become more of a man; however, it was harder on my back and stringy muscles. This was a way of life on a mountain farm, and I didn't give hard work a lot of thought as life was enjoyable. When my children grew up in town and complained about having nothing to do or being bored, I would suggest we could buy a farm and let them have an endless field of corn to hoe, for I could guarantee they would never be bored or without something to do. They never seemed very enthusiastic about the idea.

There were about 200 acres along the Hickory Flats in Grandfather's farm, and most of it was cleared and cultivated except for the hillside fields which were used as pasture for the cows, horses and other farm animals. He raised a lot of wheat, oats and buckwheat, as well as corn, potatoes and other garden products. Although Grandfather surveyed most of his working years, he seemed to have continued to farm as much as ever through the years. This was still true when I was old enough to remember the farm, but I am not sure who did most of the farm work. He was still active and was able to hire work "hands," but I don't remember these extra helpers much. There were several grandsons who helped with the farming, and I remember helping him a lot. His farm was only half a mile from our house, so it was easy for him to telephone for us to come over.

Grandfather Nutter was a serious, careful worker, and he wanted things done right. His corrections would be strict and serious, but they were usually sprinkled with a little humor, and it was easy to make him laugh with either a funny or dumb remark. This made it fun to work for/or with him.

Like all the other Nutter farmers of Hickory Flat Ridge, he hated what they called "filth," that is weeds and brush growing up in fence corners and uncultivated areas. Of course they couldn't have weeds in their corn, potatoes, or gardens, so these farms were always clean looking in our area. What a hard working group of people!

In our case, almost all neighbors were also good friends, including children and adults. We would see them at school functions, at church, at the store or at the mill. Maybe we would work with them on the farm as work might be exchanged, or we might work together on the country roads to keep them passable. These neighbors were tolerant of our childhood pranks, even if it were at their expense. Sometimes they would sound very stern, and then we would hear about them repeating the incidents with great glee.

We were close to our schoolmates, cousins and neighbors. The death of a neighbor from a few miles away that you might not know very well cast a shadow over the entire community for months. The person might be mentioned for years. Now a death notice about someone who might have been a close friend at one time is hardly given a thought. People live closer together now, but we are not as close in terms of neighborliness as we were in the country. Children in schools in cities today do not have as many close school friends as we had, for children are bussed in from other areas, and they just don't get acquainted.

I never quite understood when I was growing up the love for farm life our city cousins had. One cousin, who was later County Superintendent of Schools in Nicholas County, loved to spend his summers with Aunt Fanny and Uncle Willis Beckner. Even when he was a star athlete in high school he loved to spend his summers at their farm, which was two miles from the nearest neighbor. He would work at farming all summer with Uncle Willie, helping him load produce on a jolt wagon and drive a team three miles into town to peddle it, jolting all the way to town and back. He loved every minute of it. Maybe it is the difference in contriving fun and having enjoyment from things which come naturally, even learning to enjoy looking forward to the cold winter days or the coolness of the late, cool, cool summer evenings.

At both farms I especially remember the great food, from the gardens and fruit trees. No one appreciates good food more than an ever-hungry farm boy who has worked for hours out in the mountain air and is truly hungry, just as someone who is really cold appreciates a warm fire.

Except for a few short years, grandfather's farm has remained in the family since 1850. John Nutter bought the farm that year, and the house was built late in the 1850's. He and his wife lived there until his death in 1893. In the late 1890's my Aunt Rosa and Uncle Marvin O'Dell lived there until about 1908. My grandparents, Isaac and Mary Etta (Walker) Nutter, lived on the Deitz farm until 1908. Then they bought my parents' home at Hominy Falls, and my parents bought Grandfather's home. At that time my grandparents moved to the Noah Nutter farm at Snow Hill. A couple of years later their son, Lawrence Nutter, was married and moved to the Noah Nutter farm, and my grandparents moved back to the John Nutter farm, where they remained until his death in 1935. Three or four years later Uncle Owen Nutter inherited the farm. He had worked for many years for the West Virginia Department of Natural Resources. He retired and moved back to his farm which adjoined a farm he owned and where he had lived. When he came back to the farm he began to raise Christmas trees, but when his health got bad, he sold the farms to a friend, Bill Frances, who continued to raise and sell Christmas trees. Finally Bill Frances sold the farm back to my two brothers, Lawrence and Harold, and Lawrence still owns the farm.

    A large part of my memories of Grandfather's farm is about work, but it was fun and interesting, and some of it was play and fun.

Hunting

I have never been able to explain the great enjoyment in hunting and fishing to someone who does neither, any more than an avid golfer can explain the thrill of golfing to a non-golfer.

Today I can identify with people who ask why a person would want to kill an animal and not even want to eat it. I still love to walk in the woods, but it adds so much to have a purpose, such as hunting, identifying flowers, bird watching or looking for nuts. I was always a walking hunter. When the seasons for hunting were set much later, and the leaves had fallen, the woods were no longer beautiful, and a person had to sit still to get game. A lot of the fun went out of hunting for me after that.

About fifty years ago the State Game and Fish Division set squirrel hunting season after the leaves had fallen, and I hated this, for I loved to walk in the woods to hunt squirrels. After the leaves had fallen I felt chained to one spot, for I couldn't move without being heard. One of the arguments the Game Division used was that the baby squirrels would starve if the mother squirrels were killed. An article was printed in the state magazine which quoted an "expert" as saying he had gone into the woods and had seen dozens of young squirrels which had fallen out of their dens and were too young to climb back up in the trees. Our family and our neighbors had always hunted in the country full of squirrels and had never seen even one squirrel on the ground too young to climb back up the tree from which it had fallen.

Maybe the State Game and Fish Division was right, but two adjoining states, Kentucky and Ohio, have their squirrel seasons starting in late August.

Hunting was different when I was young, almost a part of survival, as it had been back through history. The family had to have meat, and the furs which were sold were a part of family income, which was needed for things which had to be bought. Killing animals which were destroying crops was a task of necessity, and hunting for meat was also necessary, for this saved our farm animals from slaughter. It is hard for me to understand how a person can eat a steak and still look down his nose at a person who killed wild game for food. The farm animals were our friends, and the wild animals were our enemies. The old timers would call this unmitigated gall.

Then there were the mornings when the fogs hung low on Hickory Flat Ridge before the sun burned it off. Sometimes the ever-flowing breeze would start the fog slowing moving, leaving the illusion that the trees were moving through the fog rather than the other way around.

One morning I was hunting when something happened which reminded me of a wild story my father made up of a hunter who emptied his gun when a gnat started moving on his eyebrow, thinking he was shooting at a squirrel. One morning I was sitting with my back to a tree, holding my gun straight up in front of me. I was in a hickory stand which had long, straight trunks far below the first limbs. An ant crawled up my gun barrel, and I thought at first I was seeing a squirrel running up the side of a hickory tree (it was barely daylight).

The late evening was a good time to be in the woods when the trees were gorgeous with their fall colors. By dusk there would be almost total silence except for the small sounds of squirrels making their way back to their dens, jumping from the branch of one tree to the branch of another. You could almost believe you were a thousand miles from the nearest civilization except for the distant mooing of cows or the tinkle of their bells.

Hunting can be searching for anything: wild mushrooms, teaberries, "services," blackberries or game, as long as it is in the fields and woods. Not only was the beauty of the fields and woods fascinating, but the ruggedness or roughness added to the pleasure, for there was a lot of climbing up and down hills, over rock cliffs, through brambles or briers, or climbing trees for chestnuts, "services," or wild grapes. Maybe being alone with your thoughts was part of the fascination of the fields and woods. Farm children usually had a lot of time with their own thoughts while hunting, walking somewhere or working alone on the farm. Then there were those times when a horse was ridden several miles to a store, grist mill or to the blacksmith shop. There was time for solitude and thinking things through alone.

I still like to look for morel mushrooms in the spring and pick blackberries for a cobbler, even if I spend more for gasoline than the berries would cost me at a market close to home. It is a good excuse to get into the fields or woods. I have no desire to play "roughing it," for I lived that way when growing up and experienced the real thing. I have been caught out far from home and had to sleep on the ground all night, cold and hungry, so I don't do that on purpose.

Hunting, which was once a necessity, is now recreation and an expensive hobby for some.

ISAAC NUTTER FAMILY: front row - Mary Walker Nutter, Issac holding Lawrence. Back row - Owen, Betty, Rosa. Issac son of John and Elizabeth Nutter.

Nutter Genealogy

John B. Nutter was born the second of August 1824 in Nicholas County. His father, David, was 55 years old. His mother was Christina O'Dell, the 34 year old second wife of David. What the "B." was for we have not yet discovered. It is a good bet that his name was John Benjamin for at the time of his birth, his father, David was a Sunday School teacher in Bethel Church on Laurel Run and another member of the class was Benjamin Dorsey.

In October 1847, John B. married Elizabeth Pitsenbarger, the 17 year old daughter of Peter and Elizabeth Amick Pitsenbarger. Her older sister, Christina, had 5 years earlier married John B.'s brother, Grandison.

John B. purchased 200 acres of unimproved land from Nathaniel Foster in 1851. Foster had "patented" this land in 1827. One identifying land mark was a corner at "a large sugar maple near the top of Elk Knob." This is where Sugar Grove Fire Tower now stands. John and Betsy with Alfred, born 7 August 1848, and Andrew Scott, born 19 February 1850, moved to this wildwood in the winter of 1851. As mentioned earlier they lived at first in a lean-to in the hollow. They had 2 cows and 1 horse. They had their health and their love for each other. He was very robust and had a sharp axe. He set about clearing a farm three miles from the nearest neighbor.

It was here that on April 27, 1852 their daughter Priscilla was born. Priscilla was followed by a stillborn and then on August 11, 1856, by Isaac (Ike) Dowtain. (Dowtain was a Methodist preacher in this area for many years.)

Ike was nearly 5 years old before Malinda was born in 1860. She was named for John's half sister Malinda, wife of John McClung. Malinda Nutter McClung died, a young mother, at age 40. Her niece and namesake Malinda Nutter died much younger on June 8, 1862.

Johnson Floyd had been born April 7, 1862, so Betty didn't get much time to grieve for her lost baby, Malinda. In February

1864, Mahulda was born. Hulda was just over two years old when disaster struck. Alfred drowned 13th June 1866. He was taking a "stud horse to service" and the accident occurred crossing the Meadow River near Mt. Lookout. Alfred was just 55 days short of his 18th birthday.

Six months later, in January 1867, Jeremiah was born. The baby was named for John's brother who in turn had been named for their grandfather, Jeremiah O'Dell, a Revolutionary War veteran and one of the very earliest pioneers in the wilderness of Nicholas County.

John's brother, Jerry, had sold out his homestead on Hickory Flat and resettled in the Meadow River valley at Russellville. Jerry had a son born 1868 who was named Jeremiah. Each of these young Jeremiahs died in the summer of 1876.

Joseph J., who always teased, saying the "J." stood for "Jehosaphat," was born in March 1868. Joe was the last baby born to John and Betsy. Four sons and two daughters were to reach adulthood and in turn raise their own families. Those families were:

Andy married Laura Nutter on the 5th of March 1873, Laura had been born 18th September 1857, the first child of Levi and Margaret Backus Nutter. Levi was the youngest child of David and Christina. Andy and Laura built their home and raised their family on the "Sugar Tree" farm ½ mile west of Nutterville. Their children were:

Henry T. born 29 March 1874.
Marshall G. born 24 September 1876 married Esta Amick.
Felix born 23 August 1878 married Rhoda Florence Haynes.
Irvin E. born 21 October 1880 married Pearl Amick.
Effie born 22 December 188? died 7 June 1882.
Newman L. born 29 May 1882 married Lucy Amick.
Ivy born 25 July 1885 married M. D. Molette.
Ella born 6 February 1890 married Bartlett Amick (Ella died 12 October 1920 without issue).
Lena born 29 June 1896 married Bartlett Amick 19 April 1921.

Laura died the 12th May 1898. Andy was 48 years old but there were Newman, 15; Ivy, 13; Ella, 8; and Lena, 2, still at home. Andy married the 24 year old Etta Belle Haynes and started his second family. These were:

Alden born 14 December 1900 married Nina Flint.
Delbert born 6 August 1903 married Maggie McClung.
Verna born 7 April 1906 married Telford Zopp.
Ditha born 26 June 1908 married Judson Kidwell.
Garnet born 10 January 1912 married Gaylord Hudkins.
Vinita born 28 September 1916 married Samuel Hicks.

Andy died in 1927 and was buried at Sugar Grove Church.

Priscilla married John W. Burdett in August 1868. She was 16 and Johnny, a son of Mary Ann Pitsenbarger who was Elizabeth's sister, was but 18. Their family consisted of:

Elizabeth A. born 1872 married E. F. Boley.
William A. born August 1875 married Ginnetta Haynes.
James Hayden born 1877 married (no issue).
Viola Florence born 1879 married Dan Murphy (no issue).
Bertha Belle, married Jacob Pitsenbarger.
John born 1892 married (no issue).
Blanche married Charles Burns.
Elmer born 1896 married (no issue).

Priscilla died in 1913 and is buried at Sugar Grove Church.

On June 1, 1877, Isaac married Mary Etta Walker. Ike settled about ½ mile west of his father John. (In fact this home place, which today is referred to as the "Deitz Place" is the actual location of Nutterville because Betty Nutter Deitz operated the Post Office in her home.) But back to the Ike Nutter Family:

Rosetta A. born 29 March 1878 married Marvin O'Dell.
Elizabeth J. born 30 December 1879 married J. Watson Deitz.
Owen born October 1881 married Georga Morizena.
John born 6 December 1885 died 22 days later.
Lawrence born 20 October 1889 married Jeannie Flagar.

Ike died 1936 and is also buried at Sugar Grove Church.

Johnson married Elbina Katherine Nutter in October 1883.

"Aunt Kitt" was born 4th March 1862, the first daughter of Charles and Sarah Pitsenbarger Nutter. He was a son of David Nutter Junior and Sarah was a daughter of Abraham and Nancy McClung Pitsenbarger. The children of Johnson and "Kitt" were:

Emerson born 1884 married Lettie Miller.
Luther born 1886 lived 14 months.
Malissie C. born 1887 married Wes Siers.
Floyd born 1888 married Anna Miller.
Mary E. born 1891 married Shortie Davis.
John L. born 1892 died in U.S. Army Camp of flu 1918.
Isaac N. born 1894 married ???? Amick.
Pascal D. born 1896 married Rebecca Trout.
Charles A. born 1899 married Esta Amick.
James born 1901 married Ottie Haynes.
Elzada born 1903 married Otis Groves.
Lottie born 1904 married Clinton Wyatt.
Lewis born 1904 lived 3 months.
Ethel born 1906 married Raymond Miller.

Johnson died in April 1921 and was buried at Sugar Grove Church.

Mahulda married Charles L. Amick in September 1882. Charlie and Hulda migrated to South Dakota where they reared

their family:
  Minnie, married Henry Strong.
  Ira, married (1) Earne Haynes, (2) Hazel Starret.
  Elmer born November 11, 188? died August 20, 1890, married Clara Kruse.
    Grace Marie born May 16, 1890 married Scott C. Phillip.
    John born 1892 married ??.
    Victor born 1894 never married.
    Eltha (Elsie) born 1896 married C. A. (Norman) Tranger.
    Carrie born 1898 married Lee H. Hollister.
    Ethen born 1900 married ??
  Mahulda died 30 August 1933 and is the only one of John B. and Betsy's children not buried at Sugar Grove Church.
  Joseph J. married Martha Rilla Haynes in 1888. She was the oldest daughter of Joseph and Margaret Bays Haynes. Two of Mattie's sisters and two of her brothers also married Nutters. The Joe Nutter family was:
  Pina born 1890 married Everett McClung.
  Robert Erskine born 1892 married Lula Richardson.
  Maud born 1894 married Gus Halstead.
  Oscar born 1895 married Pearl Amick.
  Della born 1897 married "Leck" White.
  Molly born 1898 married Judson C. Cohernour.
  James Ota born 1900 married Arizona Jones.
  Walter born 1903 married Glenedene Burdett.
  Joseph Eugene born 1906 married Opal Cook.
  Eunice born 1906 married Onan Moore.
  Myrtle born 1909 married Ed Wheeler.
  Oliver born 1911 married Earl Amick.
  Woodrow Wilson born 1913 married Pauline Richardson.
  Joe died in 1945 and was buried at Sugar Grove Church, property that he and Mattie donated to the Church in 1893.

Wm Elam. Esuori Sir Please to take notice that I on the first day of the Superior Court of Law to be holden in and for the County of Nicholas in the month of May next I shall by my attorney move said court to award the Commonwealth Writs of prohibition to stay all further proceeding on three several judgements rendered by Wm G Fitzwater justice of the peace in the said County of Nicholas on the 20th day of January 1830 in your favour against myself David R. Jarrin two Thomas Liff John Lewinfield and Uickian Campion the one for $17.75 cents debt subject to a credit for $10 from Nov 15th 1829 also 30 cents costs the second for $18 debt and 30 cents costs and the third for $19.50 debt and 30 cents costs which three several judgements were rendered upon three several warrants subscribed to by R Kelly as justice of the peace and in support of said motion it will be insisted that the said justices of the peace were assuming to themselves a jurisdiction that did not legally and rightfully belong to them. Yours

April 13th 1830 —   David Nutter

This legal claim written by Great-Great Grandfather David Nutter in 1830 was found in the county clerks office in Nicholas County two years ago.

Russellville
April 20th, 1878.

George W. Lewis Esqr.—
 Dear Sir after my kind regards for you and yours this leaves us in helth.
 I wish to say a few words we have got them sheep and are depending on you to by them if the weather keep fine we will sheare in a short time we are or soon will be ready for that Bull, I have not built that Log fence as I have been building me a Barn but if you have of your own some forty or fifty head of yearling cattel or two year oald I will try my hand with them if you wish or if you haint got such if any of your friend how bring them on to me and I will attend to them as best I can the weather has been remarkable fine times are very close financially out with us this winter and are still so please dropus a few lines soon and let us know if you will take our sheep and about the cattle respectfully yours

John B. Nutter

Direct your Letter to Russellville Fayette County.

This is a letter written by John B. Nutter over 100 years ago and preserved by the family.

Making Maple Syrup And Sugar

The grove of maple trees must have been a magnificent sight to see! These trees had been left from a virgin forest, which had covered several level acres on top of the mountain. They were up to 120 feet tall and four to five feet in diameter near the ground. The small trees had been cleared, and there was not much underbrush, leaving the area under the trees looking like nature's cathedral, just daring man to match the beauty. In summer the trees would have covered a great shaded area as they were so close together that only a little sunshine would filter through them, making a dappled pattern on the ground. This shaded area made a cool paradise for the farm animals on a hot summer day.

When autumn came the maple leaves would turn by the millions from green to a deep scarlet, brilliant yellow or a burnt orange. When the leaves fell there were layers on the ground several inches thick. No Indian who ever lived could have slipped through them without making a sound. The winter snows would fall, covering the leaves, and they would begin to rot, joining the rotted leaves that had fallen before them for uncounted years from those trees and their ancestors. A great floor of springy, peat-like soil had been formed.

In the deep snows of winters these maple trees would be like giant cadavers, with leafless limbs stiff in the cold winds. There were no signs of animal or human life, and the shadows falling on the snow through these wooden skeletons looked tangled. On a bright sunny day the top of the snow might melt a little and then freeze again at night. If a bright sun shone on it the next day it would glisten as though covered with an unbroken sheet of shining crystal glass.

There were only a few small maple groves remaining when I was growing up, but I have helped to make or boil down maple sap to make maple syrup or maple sugar, using almost the same method the pioneers used.

Making maple syrup and sugar must have been a difficult task for the pioneers, for the time was limited when the sap was running in the trees, and a year's supply of sugar had to be made in a short time. There was a large amount of labor needed then, but with mechanization now it is not as difficult.

A spout, called a spile, was driven into the maple tree about two inches to conduct the sap into a bucket below. These spiles were handmade small branches from trees with soft centers or cores, likely to be red sumac. Hundreds of these were made during the winter months so as to be ready as soon as the sap started to rise. Wooden buckets were made from tree trunks which were about a foot in diameter, and the center was drilled or burned out. Since the buckets probably held about a gallon, the buckets would have to be emptied and replaced fairly often, so the trees had to be watched constantly. If the temperature fell, the sap flow would slow down.

Today the spiles are bought. After boring a hole a couple of inches deep into the tree the spile is inserted to allow the sap to drain into plastic tubing and flow into plastic vats. Then it flows by gravity into a still in the still house. No one has to lift a finger to carry the sap in buckets to the sugar camp, where a fire had to be kept going day and night as long as the sugar was being made. Now the stills are heated by gas or electricity, and the heat is controlled.

Excess sap can be diverted into other stills, with the excess water from the sap boiling off constantly until maple syrup is obtained. Approximately fifty gallons of sap will make one gallon of syrup, or 100 gallons of sap will make one gallon of maple sugar.

In my grandfather's time the preparations for sugar making would start in late fall or early winter with the whittling of the spiles by hand. The size would not have to be exact, and the upper side of the tapered end would be whittled flat to gather the sap.

They could not afford to buy the number of buckets needed to catch the sap, so, in addition to the way buckets were made, sometimes green blocks of wood about ten to twelve inches across were split in half, and these halves would be hollowed out with an axe, leaving the ends and sides intact, making a small trough. A vast amount of firewood would have to be cut before the snow got deep to heat the metal vats or copper kettles to boil off the sap.

In late winter and early spring the sap would begin to rise during the warm "spells." Then the trees would be bored with augurs, and the spiles would be tapped into place. The hollowed-out wooden vessels would be placed under the open end of the spiles to catch the sap, and the "boiling off" process would begin.

Teams of horses would be hooked up to pull the homemade sleds carrying wooden, open-topped barrels. The sleds were pulled among the trees, and the wooden vessels were emptied into the barrels. The barrels were emptied into the metal vats at the sugar camp, where fires were kept going under the vats, and the water was boiled off, leaving maple syrup or maple sugar.

This was a day and night operation except for changes in the weather. If the temperatures dropped much below freezing the sap would stop running until the next warm spell. This would give the workers a chance to catch up.

I am sure that most of this was made into maple sugar cakes rather than into syrup because of the storage problems. That many jars or containers were not available. Grandfather often spoke of one room of the house which was used where there were shelves piled to the ceiling with maple syrup and sugar. The sugar cakes could be converted back to syrup by adding an equal amount of water and reboiling.

I have often wondered where this huge amount of hand labor was found, but I never was curious about this when Grandfather could have told me, so I will relate what I have heard plus what I surmised.

The neighbors with sugar groves of their own would have been equally busy at the same time, but maybe a few of them did not have many maple groves and obtained what they called their "long sweetin' " from sugar cane or sorghum. There may have been orphan children whose parents died young, as many did, and these orphans were always given a place to eat and sleep, even by non-relatives. In turn they were valuable workers in the lighter tasks, even as young children. The children of the large families could be almost as much help as an adult in most phases of sugar making.

Grandfather talked with fondness about things that happened at the sugar camps, recalling the nights when the fires were kept going but the sap gathering slowed down on the colder nights. He told about the people who helped to keep the fires burning all night so the sap would continue to boil.

Sometimes late in the winter when it was time for the bears to come out of their winter dens they would be enticed or tolled by the odor of the sweet maple syrup to come near the sugar camp, but they were scared at the sight of the fire and didn't come really near.

Grandfather remembered and talked about these neighbors who came from an area not more than five miles away, and they were fascinating to him — and to me in his stories.

Things were different then, making people just living a few hollows away very odd to each other in their actual speech, unique way of speaking, their ideas and theories on religion, or even farming methods. My people had more than average education, but this could have made them seem just as different to these part-time helpers.

The great differences among people living just a few miles apart came about because many of them were new settlers to this area and had different ethnic backgrounds. Also, some of them probably liked being "characters." They liked the attention they got — they liked being "E. F. Hutton:" everybody listened when they talked, so they might add a little to a unique way of speaking. I am sure my people sounded equally strange to these people who helped Grandfather, especially my great-grandmother with her mixture of Dutch and English in her speech.

Grandfather spoke many times of the nights around the sugar camp fires as if longing for something far away and long ago.

BURDETTE FAMILY: front row left to right - John, Hayden, John Sr. holding Elmer, Priscilla, William, Blanche. Back row - Elizabeth Ann, Viola Florence & Bertha. Priscilla, daughter of John and Elizabeth Nutter.

Death Of My Great-Grandfather's Maple Grove

When I think of the death of John Nutter's maple grove, I can only think of this with sadness and regret. Knowing where this beautiful grove of twelve acres of trees stood and knowing exactly what they must have looked like, as some of them still stand in a nearby cove, leaves a permanent feeling of a great loss yet today. It is like an ever-living member of my grandfather's house still leaves a missing member in the family in which I was a part.

Just imagine that it had been left standing and the undergrowth kept clear of underbrush and dead trees, as he kept it. What an almost unmatched sight it would be yet today! Or imagine being yet able to see this virgin stand of huge maple trees, making a different awesome sight with every change of the seasons. It would show the spring awakening or "greening up," as John B. would have called it, to the full leaf of summer, to the glory of colors of autumn of the maple leaves almost never equalled by any other trees. Then would follow the cold, stark beauty of winter with the wind blowing the snow through the bare, black skeletons of these huge maples. At other times, they might be covered with sleet with the huge trunks and even small branches covered with a sheet of ice.

Of course, I understand why this grove of maples had to be sacrificed. In the years between 1875 and 1885, John B. was able to buy sugar and molasses which he could easily afford by this time. He no longer had to expend this huge amount of labor and time to accumulate a year's supply of sugar.

He also badly needed this flat, rich hilltop for farming. The loss of the beauty of the maple grove made up for by the fact that he now owned other maple trees by the thousands. He also owned two or three other maple groves. One was the hilltop where Sugar Grove Church and Sugar Grove fire tower now stand, one mile north of his farm. Another was the Sugar Grove farm one mile south. He also owned what is now the "Deitz farm" where I grew up.

In addition, John B. could stand on any of his many hilltops and could see as far as the eye could carry, miles and miles in every direction of virgin forests.

How did John B. clear this maple grove for farming? I believe that he cut a ring around each tree through the bark which caused them to die. After two or three years, they could begin to topple over during heavy winter windstorms, thus uprooting them and leaving huge root walls. Later, they would be cut up and burned.

I remember hearing my mother and grandfather speak of hearing the giant dead trees crashing to earth during the windstorms of fall and winter. Maybe never again will we see another great maple grove in our Hickory Flats country.

Working On Country Roads

By the time I was about ten years old, I was able to work outside the family farm for wages. If our corn hoeing was caught up, I might be able to help a neighbor in his corn field.

Mostly, though, extra work for wages usually was working to repair the country roads for both wagons and cars. This work could be done when the ground was too wet to work after a rainy spell.

There was a shortage to help at that time as most late teenage boys could get work cutting timber or at the mines. Therefore, if a very young boy could do the job, he was needed.

I mostly worked for a nearby neighbor named Bartlett Amick. He was our road supervisor, along with being a farmer. I worked for him both on the farm and on the road.

My first job on the road was to carry water to the older workers, along with tools. Also, I would throw loose rocks out of the roadway. The traffic caused these rocks to work to the road surface on these mountainous rocky roads — it seemed to me by the millions. Our road mostly ran along the ridges except where they had to cross a lower level to another ridge. I worked at one time or another on this road about a distance of fifteen miles.

I worked for Bartlett Amick from the time I was ten until maybe seventeen or eighteen, at times both on the road or on his farm, if I could be spared. Both he and his wife were related to me in some way, as were most of the people in our county. He called on me a lot as they had no children old enough to help on the farm. I especially remember working on the farm because of the great country food. I usually ate breakfast by 6:00 a.m. Then we would work until 12:00 noon. Away from home, there were no snack breaks. By noon we were almost ready to take a bite out of each other. Then his wife, Lena, was such a great cook of fresh garden vegetables and meats.

There were fresh buttermilk and chicken. Then there was the

hot cornbread. The taste buds of my tongue will forever be etched with this cornbread flavor. At six that evening, we had a repeat performance.

Surely, no one ever appreciated great fresh farm food like a country boy who worked six hours in the fresh mountain air without a food break.

As I grew older, my duties increased. I began to use the shovel, the mattock, the napping hammer, and the sledgehammer.

These country roads were maintained by the county. In our case, in Greenbrier County when I first worked on country roads, all of the work was done by hand, except where a team of horses was used to pull a plow to make a ditch alongside the road for water to run off beside the road. Horses were also used to haul rock to be used to fill in the low, muddy places in the road. These rocks had to be broken up with a sledgehammer to form a rock base for the low clay bottom to keep them from forming a bottomless, muddy quagmire during rainy weather.

I remember one rockpile which was six feet high and twenty-five feet across being used to fill the road in a 300-foot distance near our farm. All of these rocks had to be broken up with a sledgehammer.

Some places, this road would go uphill for as much as a mile. We would ditch the upper side for the water to run down. At some points the water had to cross the road to the lower side of the road. We had no culverts to bury so we had to build humps in the road to cause the water to cross the road. The humps would be made of dirt and rocks, with the traffic packing humps down. If it weren't too rainy, the humps would divert the water for most of the summer before they washed out. These humps made rough riding, but saved the roads from being washed out.

Sometimes large boulders would have the dirt washed from around them until they appeared to be growing higher and higher in the middle of the road. Then we would have to drill holes with a hand-held drill while a man with a sledgehammer pounded the drill. After the holes were drilled, they would be filled with dynamite, a cap and fuse placed in the dynamite, and the fuse would be lit. The fuse would be long enough so that the man who lit it could get to safety, and the boulder be broken up, with the rest of it being removed with sledges and picks and thrown over the hill.

Finally, Greenbrier County began to buy heavier road equipment such as graders, ditchers, etc. One of their projects was to widen our narrow, winding country road. We cut and removed trees and brush. Then the stumps had to be blown out with dynamite. So holes had to be drilled under them, with dynamite caps and fuses put in place. When everything was in place for a distance of one quarter to one-half mile, a couple of the men would take off running with a pocketful of matches, lighting the fuses as they went. In a few minutes, the excitement started with one explosion after another. Stumps and rocks flew through the air almost in perfect order like a daytime fireworks show. Then came the cleanup, removing stumps and rocks from the road and maybe digging out large roots.

Finally came the gasoline-powered grader widening the road and sometimes knocking over the rail fences built too close to the road. The owners would have to rebuild the fences farther away from the road.

Sometimes, if the grader failed to get a fence close to the road, one of the boys on our crew would push a few panels of rails over, saying that the boy in this family didn't have enough to do and he was helping this boy find some chores to keep him out of trouble.

At one point, our road went into Nicholas County and then at a fork of another road doubled back into Greenbrier County.

One of our neighbors living on the Nicholas County side would drive by and fuss because he couldn't work on the half mile in Nicholas County. Then after the road was widened and graded and was in real good condition, the same neighbor stopped again.

He had been driving down our new good road. He told us that we just had to do something about our road. He had just nearly hit another car head on in a sharp turn, as both of them were going too fast. He just thought it was completely our fault and he was holding us to blame for making the road too good. Did we ever enjoy this! Maybe we had never been accused of doing a job "too good" before.

At any rate, this was an enjoyable summer with a group of hard-working, fun-loving crew of people, which included some real natural comics.

Apple Trees In Our Hills

When my great-grandfather, John B. Nutter, first settled in the hills, the hills were completely covered with virgin forests. Land was cleared so a cabin and a barn could be built, and more land was cleared for farming corn, cereal crops and gardens.

Soon after the clearing of the forest for farming, the planting of fruit trees was a high priority, for the settlers needed fruit, especially apples, to survive and feed a large family. Every successful settler had an apple orchard, which was the main source of the year's supply of fruit.

I am not sure of the methods the settlers used to plant the apple trees. They had apple seed, but they may have had a type of seed bed or nursery process to assure purer reproduction of the parent trees. They may have brought some small trees with them from back east, and they surely did some grafting.

The raising of apple trees, the storing, drying and cooking of apples to save for food for the long winter's food supply was just another thing they had to learn from someone or to figure it out for themselves.

A great variety of apples was planted so they could have early apples as early as July, both for cooking and eating raw. These were the yellow transparents and the red asters. Then by August came the strawberry, with a distinct strawberry flavor, and the golden sweet, which was a favorite of mine. When it was completely ripe, or what we called "mellow," it was almost as sweet as honey.

From September until late fall there was a great variety of apples, such as the Rome Beauty, Johnson's Fine Winter, Northern Spy, Banana, Russett, and the Milam, which was a good late fall apple and was not good until frost hit it. The Milams were good when cut up and fried with the peeling still on them. We are still able to get apples from some of the one hundred year old trees on the Deitz farm now owned by my brother Lawrence.

Before canning jars became affordable and obtainable, apples were the one fruit crop that could be made to last the entire year, or at least until strawberries ripened in the late spring of the year.

Many of these apples were from trees that were one of a kind, or not many of a kind, for they had cross pollinated naturally, just as had the Golden Delicious apple tree of Clay County, W. Va. They would not reproduce naturally, but required special care as Starks did with the Golden Delicious.

The apples, along with the peaches, pears, plums and grapes (both wild and cultivated) helped to keep a country boy's endless appetite under control.

The settlers had a number of ways of preserving or storing the winter's supply of apples. They peeled, cooked and made apple sauce. They used the all-purpose, ever present copper kettle to make kettle after kettle of apple butter, with each kettle holding about fifteen gallons. Each kettle of apples was cooked all day over an open fire out in the yard and had to be stirred constantly with a wooden paddle which had a long handle. The apple butter was stored in stone jars, and the contents were covered with some kind of sealing wax, which could have been bees' wax.

The women peeled and sliced apples for drying. Then the apples would be spread out in a warm, airy place, such as the loft over the kitchen, and allowed to dry out thoroughly. Through the winter they would be cooked or made into delicious dried apple pies, everyone's favorite.

The main method of storage of apples by the settlers was the root cellar. I barely remember a storage place used on our farm. Four huge, thick logs were flattened with an axe on two sides, then joined, forming a large rectangle. A thick layer of leaves was placed in the bottom, and the apples were poured on top of them. An even thicker layer of leaves was put on top of the apples. Then wide boards, tin, or bark was placed on top of the leaves in a manner so that the rain would run off to the sides. Apples kept real well this way.

Ways pioneers may have used apples:
1. Eating them raw
2. Stewing
3. Baking
4. Frying
5. Apple pie
6. Applesauce
7. Drying
8. Fruit salad (mixed with other fruits)
9. Sulphured apples
10. Applebutter

11. Apple jelly
12. Apple juice
13. Cider
14. Caramel apples
15. Apple tarts
16. Apple dumplings
17. Apple candy
18. Spiced apples
19. Apple-peach conserve
20. Apple salad
21. Vinegar
22. Wine
23. Apple brandy

JOHNSON NUTTER FAMILY: left to right back row - Mary, Malissia, John, Rev. Barnett, Kathrine. Center row - Mrs. White, Johnson, Sarah. Front row - Pascald, Jimmie, Charley, Zada, Lottie, Ethel. Johnson, son of John and Elizabeth Nutter.

Raising And Shearing Sheep

The raising of sheep among the early settlers was an important part of surviving in the early days and continued to be until the industrialization of the country.

Sheep required a lot of care as they are almost defenseless against predators such as bears, wolves, and sometimes even domestic dogs. Lambs are defenseless against foxes.

The early settlers kept their sheep inside strong fields and inside animal-proof barns at night. They trapped wolves and bears with traps and wolf pens. They kept hunting dogs which helped keep these animals at a distance and trailed them for the hunters to shoot.

Birth control for the lambs was practiced by settlers so that the lambs would not be born until warmer spring weather came as a new-born could not survive the cold mountain winters. This was accomplished by penning the bucks away from the ewes. Thus, romance wasn't stopped; it was just delayed.

Sheep were a necessary ingredient to early settlers, both for food and clothing, and as a cash crop. Every early settler's home contained a loom, a spinning wheel, and knitting needles. The amount of labor done by these mountain women to wash the wool, to make cloth on the loom, to spin on the spinning wheels, and then to knit; the click of the knitting needles went on every minute of sitting time, making the only music heard in many a mountain cabin for hours on end.

In addition, the cloth was dyed with dye obtained from hulls from nuts and the bark of trees and poke berries.

We raised sheep on our farm in about this same way. We no longer had to worry about the wolves and bears killing the sheep, but we still had the problem of foxes killing the new-born lambs. We still had to worry about skeep-killing dogs. Farmers always destroyed these dogs, but dogs from nearby villages might run wild and become sheep-killers. The farmers would then hunt and try to destroy these dogs.

In spite of the precautions, sometimes a lamb would be born early and raised in a warm spot, maybe in a box behind the kitchen stove and fed milk in a baby's bottle. Often, they would end up a pet. They made great pets although they might be bossy, spoiled brats. They are called cossets. As they grew older, they would seem to adopt one member of the family and would follow them everywhere.

Usually, we kept forty or fifty sheep. They had to be cared for and looked after carefully. Usually, they were kept in a fenced field with a water trough. From early spring until late fall, they could graze in the open fields with the rams kept in a separate small field. In the spring and summer, the lambs were fun to watch as they were very playful animals. They liked to race and jump stiff-legged or butt heads.

When the weather got warmer in late spring, they had to be sheared. We usually hired a neighbor woman to do this as she needed the money. She happened to be a small woman and needed someone to lift the sheep to a platform to be sheared. There it would be tied down, and she would shear one side from the upper legs to the backdown. Then it had to be turned and the other side sheared, with the wool put in a large eight-foot-long sack. It would be sold for cash as we no longer spun, wove, or made cloth, but bought most of our clothes, except for enough yarn to knit socks, toboggans, and mittens.

The sheep shears used were similar to scissors, except that they were larger and shaped so that the tension of the steel would cause them to spring back open after each clip made.

One thing I remember about this lady sheep-shearer was one time my mother asked her if she ever had extra eggs for sale. Her answer was, "Yes, sometimes. No, not often." I think we kids used this answer for almost everything for years afterwards.

When late fall and winter came, we had to really care for the sheep. They spent the winter in our big open flat field on top of the hill. Stacks of straw or hay were kept here for them to feed on, but had to be specially constructed so that the whole haystack wouldn't slide down the pole and smother them after they had eaten their way all of the way from the outside to the pole in the center.

They also had to be given salt often.

It was one of my chores to check on them every day, both on my way to and from school. Often this hilltop field would have snow blowing sideways, with the ever-blowing winds coming all the way from the Western Plains.

Sometimes, I would have to break paths to the watering troughs. This was my favorite job, with the rougher the weather being the most fun. I knew every sheep and gave each one a name. What a rugged, beautiful field this was, being able to see the view for miles.

Sheep were a very valuable cash crop. In addition to the wool, lambs were sold to buyers in the fall of the year for the market. The buyers would come through and buy all of the lambs or sheep and then hire neighborhood boys and then, along with trained sheep dogs, drive them to market or railroads fifteen or twenty miles away.

Sheep would also be butchered for food the year round. Farmers tanned their own sheep skins and almost every home had a large sheep skin on every chair in their living room in front of the fireplace. It was a wonderful feeling to come in from a cold, snowy, wintry day and sit on a sheep skin-covered chair in front of a big, roaring fire.

JOE NUTTER FAMILY: left to right front row - Otie, Walter, Eunice, Eugene. Seated - Mattie, Joe, Mertie on Mattie's lap. Back row - Mollie, Oscar, Della, Maud, R.E., Pina. Joe, son of John and Elizabeth Nutter.

Hog Butchering

In our country Thanksgiving Day was not a day of food and fun. It was a working day. Usually it was hog butchering day. Before the days of refrigeration, hog butchering had to wait until the weather was cold enough to save our winter's supply of meat, along with salt-curing. I know that many of you are old enough and remember the same things if you grew up in the country. Maybe this will help you remember.

Hog butchering day, usually Thanksgiving Day, was usually that day with us. The day started about daybreak. A home-made sled was our scraping, scalding platform. An open topped barrel would be anchored and leaned at an angle, the top just above the sled platform and filled with water. A fire would be started on rocks heated in the fire, then dropped into the barrel of water, then removed and reheated in the water until the water was hot enough. Hot enough was when you could dip a finger quickly three times, but four times would blister your finger. A hog would be shot with a .22 rifle and bled.

When I was ten or eleven years old, I became the shooting expert for the family, my grandfather, and even some neighbors, as my older brothers were gone from home but they had taught me the exact shooting spot and angle. My father just seemed to assign this job to the boys in the family.

The hog would then be dragged onto the platform and slid into the barrel of hot water to loosen the hair. It would be dragged from the barrel to the sled platform.

Two or three people would start scraping hair from the hog with butcher knives by the hand-full, the hog being dipped into the hot water again and again every few minutes until the carcass was scraped clean of hair. The carcass would then have a two-inch pointed stick between the hind legs between the bones and tendons. The carcass could then be slid up a thick pole, set at an angle, until the carcass would be completely off the ground upside down. A tub would be placed under the carcass and the body would be split the length of the body on the belly side from the throat all the way down. Then a tub would be placed under the hog's nose to catch the intestines or "innards," as the old settlers would call them. Special delicacies would be separated and kept, such as the liver, the heart, the kidneys, and the lungs, or "lights," as they often called them.

Fat or lard from the intestines would be rendered or stripped from them, as well as from other parts of the carcass. The winter's supply of lard was thus obtained. Strips of lean and fat would be cut and ground into sausage on a hand-turned sausage grinder. Many people turned the intestines wrong side out and washed them many times, then stuffed them with meat for wieners, etc. Parts from the head would be used to make "head cheese" or souse. This would be placed in stone jars and eaten without further cooking.

The rest of the carcass would be cut into shoulders, hams, bacon, sidemeat, pork chops, etc. The shoulders, hams, sidemeat and sow belly would be stored in a cold building or meathouse with a thick layer of salt covering each part to preserve it along with the cold, cold weather. Sometimes these parts would be smoked for flavor and preservation.

Sausage-making was a long, hard working job when several hogs were slaughtered. Much of this work was done by the girls in the family. The sausage was ground by a sausage grinder turned by hand. Sometimes tubs full of sausage would be ground up. It would be partially cooked and preserved in mason jars with grease or lard poured over it and the lids tightened. Pork chops would also be kept this way.

I remember times after I had come to work in Charleston helping my father-in-law butcher hogs. He had moved to a small farm near town and would sometimes raise a few hogs. One cold Sunday, he asked me to help him with the butchering. I took a good friend along to help, another old Greenbrier County farm boy. He showed us a trick with the sausage grinder. He anchored the grinder to a farm sled with a tub under it to catch the sausage. He then tied a string to the handle with the other end tied to the outside part of the spoke of a Model A Ford. This wheel was jacked up so the wheel was off the ground, thus running free when the motor idled slowly.

The whole day of hand turning was reduced to about one hour with a tub of sausage as the result.

The reward for the long, cold day on the mountain farm was almost made up for on the evening of the first day, with the after-dark supper of fresh sausage, eggs, and hot biscuits, as well as liver, pork chops, gravy, and the other pork which we were starved for after a six months' period without them.

It was amazing how this daylight to darkness, long, cold hardworking day faded to almost nothing when you entered a big farm house with the hot open fire place, the warm kitchen, the dining room table piled full of piping hot food, the cooking odors making it seem impossible to find time to wash up before eating.

After all, no one ever, ever appreciates food like a country boy who has worked outside all day on a cold, gray day.

AMICK FAMILY: left to right - Victor, Theodore (son of Jacob Amick of Sioux City) C.L.'s older brother, C.L., Minnie, Mahulda, Ernie (Haynes) Ira's wife, Carrie, Elsie, person by proch is probably John, Ira by his Overland car.

Victor, Minnie, Carrie, Elsie, John and Ira are children of Mahulda (Nutter) and Charles L. Amick. Other children not in this picture were Elmer and Grace, they were married and not sure where Ethan was. Picture taken Dec. 1916.

Honey

From the very first settlers to present days, honey and the honey bees have been a valuable asset.

In the early days, honey was valuable for food and sweetening for other foods. The wax from the honey comb was used in many ways but was especially valuable to seal and, therefore, save many food products stored in stone crocks and other vessels.

The bees yet today serve for the pollination of all fruits and vegetables.

At first the pioneers got their honey by finding the hollow (usually gum) trees that held the bees and honey. They cut these trees and then cut into the hollow place which held the honey. The trees which held the honey were found by following the "bee lines" from the blossoms to the bee "gum." They would watch the bees rise into the air, turn a little, and then follow a straight line toward their home or hive. A small amount of honey or molasses would then be placed at spots some distance away. When the bees found this, they would then go to the honey or molasses, rise and make the "bee line" back to the hive. This way a person could tell where the straight lines would meet, and the tree the bees entered could be found. The tree was then cut, and the bees were robbed of their honey.

Before long the pioneers decided to have a steady source for honey by providing bee hives by saving the part of the tree that was the home of the bees, so they cut off the part of the tree below the knot hole where the bees entered and left the tree. They would cut far enough below the entrance and the hollow place where the wood was solid. They tried to saw so that this would make a square base, and the bee hives would stand up straight on a base they would provide. Another cut would be made about five feet up at a slight angle and into the hollow part of the tree. After moving this section of the tree to where they wanted it, usually near the house, a board would be sawed which was wider than the hive, and it would be placed on top on the angle cut, providing a roof which allowed the rain to run off the top.

When the hive filled with honey in mid-summer, the wide board would be taken off, and the bees would be robbed of part of their honey. The top board was then replaced. Part of the honey would always be left in the hive, and there was enough summer time left for the bees to refill the empty space, providing the bees food for the winter months.

The felling of the tree, the moving of their home and the robbing of the honey could create more colonies of bees, as swarming might take place.

The pioneers began to provide extra homes or hives for the bees by cutting out hollow sections of the gum trees, squaring the solid bottom and providing a board top. This piece of the hollow tree was placed near the other bee hives. Sooner or later the older colonies of bees would breed a new queen, thus having two queens in one hive. When this happened, one of the queens would leave the hive, with half the colony following her. This was called swarming.

The settler would try to capture this newly formed colony by tolling them to the empty home, sometimes with honey or molasses. If the queen could be captured and placed in the new home, the colony would follow her, thus forming a new hive.

I can remember when almost everyone still called bee hives "bee gums," long after sections of the gum trees had been replaced by manufactured hives with special wooden frames in the top. These frames could be removed, robbed of their honey and replaced without disturbing too many of the bees.

Everyone who had orchards kept bees to pollinate the fruit trees. The bees carried the pollen from the fruit tree blooms, clover and anything else that bloomed to make honey, carrying the pollen on their feet and depositing it on the honey comb in the hive. The honey carried the flavor of the tree blooms they fed on, and the color of the honey, from dark to golden, was also determined the same way. The favorite flavors of the settlers was from the linden and sourwood trees. This honey was light in color. They also liked the honey from fields of clover.

The wax from the honey comb was often mixed with lard or tallow and used as a water repellant, and it was also used to make candles.

I grew up with bee hives all around the farm, and I was one of the people who was hardly ever stung by honey bees. I once helped to retrieve a swarm of bees by climbing up the trunk of a tree for about fifteen feet and sawing off a small limb where they had swarmed. I then slid down the tree trunk without receiving a sting. I didn't have any netting to protect me.

My nephew told me an interesting story about a swarm of bees that alighted under the ledge of the drug store where he was the manager. This was in the Washington, D.C. area. Someone called a nearby bee keeper who came with a ladder, got the queen bee along with some other bees, and placed them in a bee hive. The rest of the colony followed them into the bee hive.

After stopping up the entrance to the hive, the man placed the hive in his truck and drove off. Hundreds of spectators watched from the parking lot. Many of them took pictures of the whole operation and were fascinated as almost no one had ever seen anything like this.

Bee keeping for honey production is a means of making a living for several hundred persons living in Appalachia today and is a hobby for others. According to the Department of Agriculture, the largest number of bee keepers in West Virginia is in the Eastern Panhandle, but there are about 5,000 bee keepers in the state.

Alexander David Deitz

Alexander David Deitz is our fourth grandchild and third grandson. I am choosing him to write about only because I was able to keep him one winter. The lady who stayed with him became ill and his mother taught school. I was happy to have this time with him. Alex had a habit of getting up when his brother, George, went to school. He would come downstairs, lie on the couch to watch what he called his channel on TV, and he would soon go back to sleep. I would decide to watch some other station and Alex would wake up and say, "That's not my channel." I would then change it back to where he wanted it and he would soon be asleep. I would try again, but he would always wake up and say, "That's not my channel." During the whole year, I was never able to get away from his channel so I finally conceded.

When Alex was about eighteen months old, his "dad's" dad (Grandfather) took him and his brother, George, to Camden Park to enjoy the day with the rides, etc. Soon Alex became thirsty. He spied a water fountain and the pictures show him trying to solve the problem of how to get a drink out of a water fountain. It was a challenge for him.

Sometimes in the afternoon before George came home from school, Alex and I would drive somewhere. One day before getting in the car, I thought one of the tires looked low, so I kicked the tire. From that time on Alex always had to walk all the way around the car, kicking all four tires before he would get in the car. He would then say, "Us go now."

We often went back to the Deitz farm (picture of house on front of book) through the years. When Alex was a little older, we took him and his brother, George, up for a week. My, how that little fellow loved the farm! Every night Alex hated to go to sleep, afraid he would miss something. He would go to bed with me. I would read and he would take a picture book to look at. Every few minutes he would ask Mom "mom's" (Grandmother), "Are you awake?"

He loved everything about the farm. His favorite past-time was riding on his grandfather's lap while mowing the grass. This yard had to be the best-mowed one in the state as Alex saw spots that had been missed, thus giving him another chance to ride on the mower.

My brother-in-law had brought a tractor to the farm and each day Alex wanted to take a ride on what he called the truck. We told him we didn't have a key for it; from then on each day he talked about the farm and asked if we had a key for the truck.

When the school year ended, our son and his wife moved to the Panama Canal Zone. Alex continued to ask about the farm. When they flew home two years later on vacation, Alex told his mom and dad he wanted the plane to let him off at the farm, asking George to stop off with him. When the plane landed in Pittsburgh near his mother's home, he was an upset little boy!

After the family moved to the Canal Zone, Alex started to nursery school. One day the teacher had a show-and-tell session. Alex took his all-time favorite record, "The Little Drummer Boy," to show. Somehow the record was lost. Alex never let his teacher, Mrs. Walker, forget this. Alex told George that when Mrs. Walker would tell him to be quiet and not talk so much, as he sounded like a motorboat, he would then ask her about his Little Drummer Boy record until Mrs. Walker just wouldn't say anything to him.

One time he got sick during the night and had to be taken to the hospital to see the doctor. When they returned home, his mother told him he wouldn't have to go to school and could sleep in since he had been awake most of the night. Alex said, "For goodness sake, tell Mrs. Bellgrave (the housekeeper) as she will gripe, gripe, gripe, all day long!"

Alex's mother, Nikki, calls him the big spender in the family and will have to have a way to make a million dollars per year in order to survive. His brother, George, tells how he has tried to get Alex to pool their allowances for birthday and Christmas presents through the years, but made no headway for Alex always thought there must be another way to have the money for gifts without using his allowance.

On the last day of one of their vacations, I happened to stop where they could play the game machines. Alex was thrilled with those games! We agreed that we would both save our quarters for the next vacation two years away to play again. During the next two years when we talked on the phone, we would ask how many quarters each had saved. Alex's answer was always a little vague. Two years later when they drove up in front of the house, Alex asked his mother for a quarter and when she asked him why he needed it, he said, "I can't go in without any money at all for the game machines for Mom "mom's" (Grandmother) thinks I have been saving up for them." Of course, when he came in he wanted to know, before I could ask him, how much money I had saved.

Alex is now fourteen years old and six feet tall and growing up. The thrill of the farm, the rides at the park, and the game machines are now in the past. We are now in the computer stage. Time waits for no one, but memories last forever.

By Madeline Deitz

An Interesting Challenge

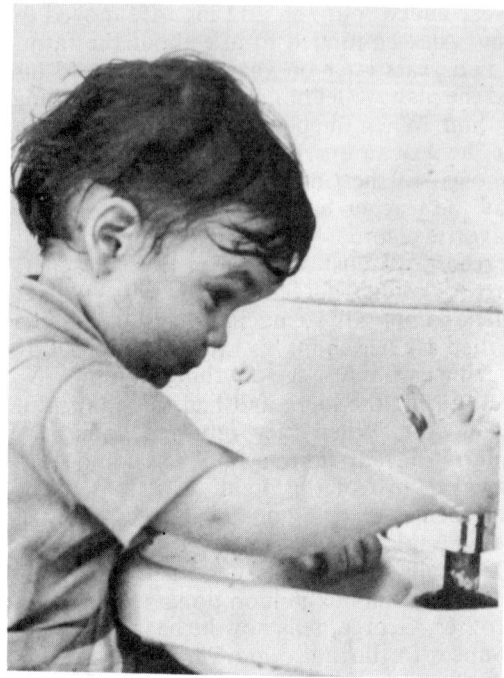

BIG ATTRACTION at Camden Park for 18 month-old Alex Deitz was the mysteries of a water fountain. A very determined young lad, Alex spent quite some time trying to figure out how to adjust the flow of water so that he could get a drink. Alex is the grandson of Dennis Deitz.

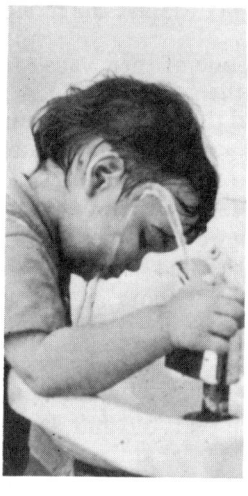
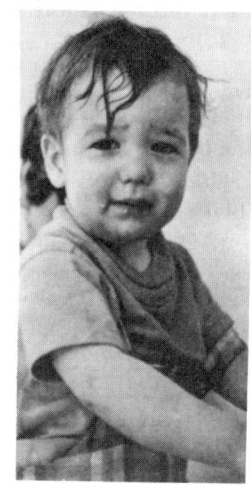

It Took Awhile...But Alex Got That Drink of Cool Water

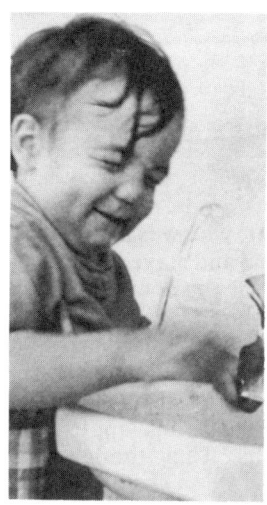
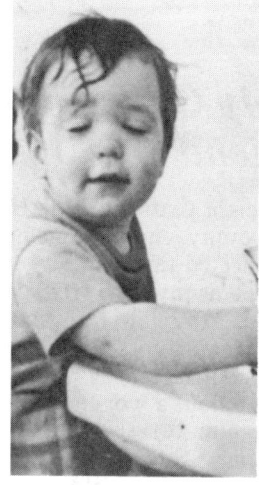
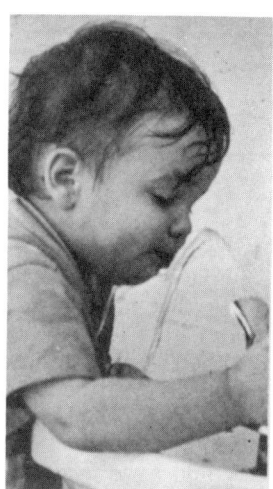
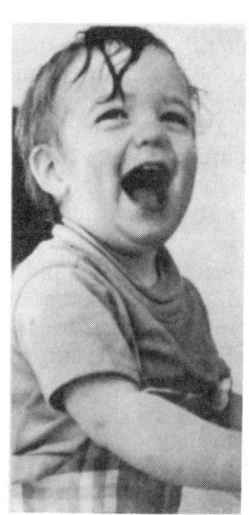

My Childhood Friend And Hero

Until I was about eight years old, Bob Hunt, who was a deputy sheriff in Greenbrier County, came to our house and stayed two or three days while he collected taxes in that end of the county.

The family said he was my hero from the time I was a toddler and tried to stay on his lap while he was trying to collect taxes. When I was just three or four years old, he came late at night after I had gone to bed. I got up the next morning, dressed and came downstairs went over without a word and climbed on his lap, even though I hadn't seen him for several months. They thought I would have forgotten him.

When I was about eight years old, he sold out and moved to Ohio, and I never saw him again, but I have never forgotten him. I wonder how long he lived, where he moved to in Ohio, and where his children are today.

Many years later some of the family met Bob Hunt when he was on a visit back to Greenbrier County, and the first person he asked about was me. I was so proud. I still thought that if Bob Hunt had lived in Missouri after the Civil War that Frank and Jesse James would never have dared to leave their cave.

In the evenings Bob Hunt would sit around the fire and tell wild, wonderful stories about being a deputy sheriff and arresting dangerous outlaws in faraway places. Later I realized that these outlaws had probably stolen a small tool, and the far-a-way places I could only imagine were about fifteen miles from my home. I just couldn't believe that anyone would be foolish enough to break the law knowing that my Superman, Bob Hunt, would be on his trail. I remember the thrill of seeing him ride up, a big handsome man on a beautiful horse. I knew I would get to listen to his stories of his experiences and about the strange people he knew in our county. Years later I probably met and knew many of them. At that time, in my imagination, they were as strange to me as a visitor from Mars would be today.

The robbery of the Bank of Rupert, Bob Hunt's territory, was the biggest story of all. Later, around the fireplace, I heard a play by play account of the hunt for the robbers.

I was fascinated when he told of getting bloodhounds, helping follow the trail of the robbers, of seeing them at one point, and then nearly catching them. In those mountains, the deputies could not go as fast as the robbers, for they could only go as fast as the bloodhounds followed the trail, and they had to hold on to the leashes as the robbers would shoot the bloodhounds if they were turned loose.

Later the robbers were caught as they were dumb enough to leave a lot of evidence as to their identities. They just had to be that dumb, or they would never have committed a crime in my hero's territory.

As I grew older, other versions of the robbery and chase began to be told and written, which sounded more like the Keystone Kops. One of these versions follows.

Christina O' Dell Nutter
Born 1790 - Died 1891
Mother of John B. Nutter

The Rupert Bank

By Louis A. Childress
From The *West Virginia Hillbilly*
Vol. 10, No. 30 — July 26, 1969
Richwood, W. Va.

The Childress family hunting party, of which my father had been the nucleus since the turn of the century and Yew Pine Mountain forays, was encamped about one mile up Clear Creek from Rupert on the property of Mrs. Yocum, one of whose daughters was the wife of Al Yewell, a member of our party. All the older members of father's party were gone, but he had plenty of younger friends and family who joined, and seven of us, cousins and close friends, had taken over the logistics of the camp operation.

This 15th day of September 1921 I had hunted half exploring and sightseeing, to the top of the mountain . . .

Cappy Wise, a county road engineer, remarked he was taking his Ford car, one of four in camp, down to the new garage for some minor repair, and did anyone want to go along for the ride. Two of us did and we drove off.

In 1921 Rupert consisted of the Rupert General store and post office, the Rupert residence, and a small tin-sided building 50 yards or more west of the store, which contained the bank of Rupert. The town showed hopes of boom though, everyone could see that. The railroad from Rainelle was just completed, and the first locomotive had arrived in Rupert just two or three days before. The name of the optimist who built the first building in new Rupert I have forgotten, but the edifice was a garage, built about 300 yards up the Clear Creek road from Route 60 in a dense woods of second growth white oak. The present highway from Rainelle to Rupert was under construction; the grade was completed only a day or so before this, but was impassable on account of mud. All traffic still used the old turnpike over Little Sewell Mountain, which was dry and not bad at all, a half mile or so of corduroy east of the mountain foot. The entire route down Meadow River from Rupert to Rainelle was through solid woods. There may have been one habitation a little east of present Charmco then, but that would be the only one. In

Rupert the entire north side of the road was woods to some yards east of the Clear Creek road, which came into Route 60 where it does now. The Clear Creek road was quite crooked through the white oak woods, and vision was limited to a few yards at any point.

This new garage was two story, built of new lumber, the upstairs finished as a living flat, in which the proprietor lived, but there was no siding on the first floor of the garage. He had installed a work bench, and necessary machinery on the dirt floor, and was open for business to help finish his building program. We drove to the man's place and he went to work and soon had the trifling task completed. As we waited we could hear the rural telephone upstairs ringing frequently, and as rural telephones were only a gigantic party line, all housewives took down the receiver and listened.

Presently the man's wife screamed his name, and before he could answer, she shrieked for him again. By this time he had run out through the unfinished side of the garage where he could look up and see what she wanted. She called as loudly as she could yell, "The bank has been robbed." None of us believed it. Banks just were not robbed back there in 1921. The Bonnies and Clydes had not come along. The last bank robbery had been a half mythical thing in Huntington during the seventies, and nobody believed it could happen now.

Seeing doubt in our faces, the wife said, "I just heard the bank cashier talking to the Sheriff's office in Lewisburg. He told the sheriff to come at once."

Had it not been for the thick growth of trees we could have looked straight into the bank's front door from where we stood. We all leaped into the car and headed for the bank. The little building stood perhaps 50 yards west of the Clear Creek road junction, we rounded it and stopped in front. It had hardly been five minutes since the robbery and we were the first persons on the spot. A covered porch ran across the front of the building on which three men stood with set expressions on their faces as if still in trauma. One was the cashier, the other two were loafers in the bank and witnesses to the hold-up. The garage man with us knew the cashier and spoke to him. The man pulled himself together and slowly told us what happened.

It was almost closing time, when suddenly three masked men sprang through the door, pushed a cocked revolver in the face of each man present, scooped up $1,050 and some change, ran out across the road and into the woods on the north side of the highway. Maybe we had seen them as we came down through the woods, the banker said hopefully. We said, no. While we waited, the sheriff called to say he hoped to make Rupert before night with a dog man and bloodhounds. There ought to be a posse, said the cashier. Half a dozen other persons had arrived by this time. We said we would go back to camp, get supper, and return by the time the sheriff arrived. At supper, when we had outlined the tentative plans, Yewell said he would go with us. "I have had quite a lot of experience with blood hounds, and I know the dog man will need some help."

We arrived at the bank well before dark. A car soon drove up and out stepped the sheriff, a Mr. McClung, 65 years old, tired looking, dressed in overalls and a sweat stained shirt, with a double barreled shot gun in the crook of his arm. The cashier repeated the simple story, showed where the robbers crossed the road and jumped the two-foot bank on the northside of the road and disappeared into the woods. Mr. McClung asked that none of us walk in that area until we were organized and ready to go. A conference was held in the middle of the road, theories were advanced as to who would have perpetrated the crime, but a general sense of bafflement prevailed. We strangers kept quiet because we knew nothing of the local people. When all had had their say, an elderly man, apparently older than the sheriff, with snow white hair and mustache, stepped between the sheriff and the cashier and said:

"Men, I have heard all that has been said here, and I have an idea who you are looking for. I think I know who did this. There are three of them. They won't work, and they are just dumb enough to pull such a trick. They live out on the ridge. Several men here know where they live. I say let about six men slip away from here in one of these cars, but stop about a mile from the house, wait till dark, slip up and lie down near the house, and about midnight or before they will walk right into your arms." The sheriff was a stranger to the people of this district, and was unfamiliar with the geography. Also, the cashier seemed to know nothing of the three suspects named by the old gentleman, who was carrying an old-fashioned barn lantern. I'll call him the "lantern man" because I have forgotten his name. It was now nearing dark. The sheriff went to the car and told the dog man to prepare. Al Yewell had already introduced himself to the dog man and they had talked dogs while the conference was on. I had no faith whatever in blood hounds, knowing nothing about them beyond what I had read in Uncle Tom's Cabin, of the hounds chasing Eliza across the floating ice of the Ohio River. These dogs bore little resemblance to hounds of any kind I had ever seen. They were too large for hounds, weighing somewhere between 75 and 100 pounds each, and were patently some kind of mongrel mix, with a slight touch of hound color. Each dog had a large strong collar, to which was attached a stout chain, ending in a harness leather hand loop.

The sheriff now addressed us, "Men, I deputize all of you to constitute a posse to help me catch these robbers." He signaled to the dog man to take up the track. The dogs were let out of the car, and the dog man handed one lead to our man Yewell and the two of them led the dogs a few yards to the edge of the woods. The sheriff selected six from the 30 or so assembled, and told the rest to proceed slowly along the road for the time being. The sheriff, an old man, was taking the rough mountain track while the road was full of young strong men. One of them said, "Why don't you fellows who own this Ford drive it along the road? There are enough of us to carry it through the bad places if necessary, and we can spell the old sheriff by letting him ride."

Cappy Wise said, "Sure, we will. Louis and I will take turns driving."

We were moving slowly along what is now Route 60, toward Rainelle, and from what the natives said, this would be the first car over this piece of road. The road grade was largely yellow clay, and there is no question but what it is slicker than red clay when wet. We could hear the woods party on the mountain side, and it was easily observable that the track (no one said trail all night) was going down Meadow River toward Rainelle. I observed the lantern man trudging along, and with difficulty persuaded him to get into the car and blow his lantern out and ride. He was easily the oldest man in the posse, maybe 75 or older. He refused until assured there were plenty of matches in the crowd to relight with.

Now down the hill came the sheriff with a young man escort. Two fresh men at once took over up the hillside to replace them. The sheriff brought news. Out of his pocket he pulled several coins and a crumpled dirty dollar bill. He said the dogs had nosed this money out of the leaves over a half mile distance, where the robbers had divided up the money as they walked along. This confirmed that we were on the right track, and according to his native advisers, the robbers were headed for Rainelle, several miles away. We told the sheriff that he might as well ride and rest awhile, for which purpose we were bringing the car along the new road grade. Within an hour after the sheriff joined the road contingent, the old lantern man asked the sheriff to stop the posse at this point for a while and let him look for tracks. We did, and he lit his lantern. He started down the river bank looking carefully at the ground as he went. Here was a scattering of large stones in the river, close enough together so that an active person could cross the river dry shod, by leaping from stone to stone. The natives and hunters used this place to cross the river. One of the party said this crossing led straight to the habitation of the suspects the old man had named.

After scouting for about 10 minutes, the lantern man came back to the road and said, "Well, they haven't crossed here. They are going to Rainelle. You men are in for a long night, and I think I'll just walk back home from here and get to bed."

At this point it was at least five miles back to Rupert, plus whatever distance from there to his home. We tried to persuade him to accompany us and stay in the car, and we would eventually take him home. He said he was used to walking, and he would be home by the time we got to Rainelle. Five minutes after we left the river crossing we came to what the men said was the worst place in the road. Cappy, who was driving, stopped the car, and we all looked the mud hole over. It was about 30 yards long, the worst part immediately where we would enter it, growing shallow toward the western end.

We planned that the driver of the empty car would start ten feet back from the edge of the mud hole, with the car in low gear with wide open throttle, and the rest of us would seize the car at the edge of the mud and push hard, never letting it slow down if we could prevent it, and ram it right on to the hard ground at the other side. This worked perfectly except for a mishap to one of the pushers. Addison Shepherd, a contemporary of my father's and his guest on the hunt, said at the supper table he believed he would go with us. He had heard all his life about posses and their chases but never had an opportunity to join one before, and he would go along for the excitement. Although he was 50 years old, we knew he was a good walker because he was a great quail hunter. He could not drive a car, and knew nothing about them except you could ride in them faster than a buggy. We had put the top up on the Ford before we left camp as we did not know what the weather might be that night. With the top up, the top bracket which held the folded top down made an inviting hand-hold for the pusher. Shepherd grabbed this fixture when the car roared by us, and gave some good pushing, but as the car's wheels got traction, the car leaped forward, and as Shepherd's hand had become caught in the bracket, he was jerked from his feet and towed like a log, head first through 30 or 40 feet of soupy yellow clay before the car stopped on solid ground. He was the most terrible looking object known to man. We stood him up in the glare of the car lights, and Cappy came forth with a double handful of clean machinists waste, and we started wiping his eyes out first, then his cheeks and forehead. The mud had not only covered him but went down his collar, under his belt and partially filled the inside of his pants. He was a good sport about it all; his hand was slightly bruised, and after wiping his hands, he lighted a cigar and said he was alright. He said he had been wet and muddy many a time, and "now let's get on with the chase."

We could hear the woods party forging slowly along, and I must say when the sheriff joined us back there with the salvaged money, my opinion of blood hounds underwent a swift change, for I had looked for dropped things in deep leaves enough to know that the dogs nosed the light objects. Now we moved on roughly, parallel to the woods party. The sheriff said he believed he would go back and join them, but two of our men said for us to wait. If the culprits were actually going to Rainelle they would soon come down off the hill and cross the river on the new bridge a mile or two ahead, and if that occurred, the hill group would come back to the road at that point. Looking back, from this distance, I believe all the more experienced local men with us had in mind the unspoken belief we were tracking the old lantern man's suspects, but since the sheriff, the dog man, the Kanawha County delegation, which was us, were uninformed about the local situation, nothing was said.

Soon we saw the lights of the woods party coming slanting down the hill to the road, and they joined us at the east end of the concrete bridge about two miles east of Rainelle. It was new then and unused because the road had been impassable. You now drive from Rupert to Rainelle in 10 to 12 minutes, and it may be hard to believe we had been about five hours making it to this bridge. Now I saw how the dogs worked. Each was pulling hard on his man, and after the rough passage around the mountain side, the men were fagging out. We worked straight along the road. About 28 men, a car and two big dogs. A teenage boy ran out on the porch, took one look and sprang back into the house shouting, "The posse." Two men and the boy joined us at once, each armed with some sort of gun. When we left camp it had not occurred to a single one of us to bring a gun. We simply considered ourselves visitors. It had not occurred to us to bring any food either, which was a mistake. Cappy had two of his oranges in the car, so we divided them and ate them. If you ever join a posse, don't forget the food.

We were now passing an almost continuous row of houses, and at each the scenario was the same as the first. Someone ran out to see, leaped back into the house, grabbed guns, and by the time the new road joined the James River and Kanawha Turnpike in Slabtown, now East Rainelle, 200 men and boys armed with guns, butcher knives and more than one carrying scythe blades, made up our posse. This bunch may not have scared the enemy, but, by George, they scared me.

Now we came to the boardwalk which ran from Slabtown to the company store in the center of main Rainelle. The dogs were nosing along the walk, and I could not understand how they could keep the track where hundreds of others had recently walked. Half of the population of Rainelle was with us now, and we were no longer a posse, we were a pedestrian assembly. The entire countryside had heard long ago of the robbery and that a posse was out, but not a person present had dreamed the posse would come to Rainelle. It was the biggest thing that had ever happened in this part of the country. We moved slowly onward until at last we came to the center of Rainelle and the company store. Here the sheriff called a halt, and the dog man explained we had lost the track back there some where near the beginning of the board walk, and we must now go back to Slabtown and try to pick it up again.

The sheriff asked the entire gathering to stay back at least 50 yards from the dogs to keep from distracting them or confusing the track. I took the dog men and the sheriff in the car and hustled back to Slabtown far ahead of the crowd. They dismounted and started in what is now the main street of East Rainelle. The dogs cast hither and yon just as I had seen bird dogs and hounds do in searching for a lead. By this time two or three hundred people gathered again behind us, the dogs had picked up a confused or mixed track which led eventually to a group of mean habitations along the foot of the hill, made of the bodies taken off box cars and set up on rickety foundations.

The dogs seemed to say, "These fellows are around here somewhere, but we can't tell just in which shanty."

I now had all our delegation in the car except our dog man, who, of course, was working with his dog. Our delegates with me agreed this was probaly "IT," and the shooting might start any minute. I looked around and saw a stack of lumber as large as a house nearby and drove the car tight in against it on the side away from the shabby shacks, and possible gun fire. There were at least 200 armed men and boys present just itching to shoot at something, and I did not want to be in the line of fire. Neither did my passengers. We sat and smoked and talked about the night and what had happened. It was now well past midnight. There was not a bite to eat that could be bought within 50 miles. No restaurants then, the stores closed, where you could get crackers and cheese, the staple emergency diet of that time. We caucused and decided to chicken out on the posse, after I had peeped out and saw the dogs on an apparently good track, straight up the road eastward up Little Sewell Mountain.

We started out, and overtaking the sheriff, informed him of our intention of leaving him, much to our regret. He thanked us and said he still seemed to have plenty of help, which was quite evident. We asked our dog man if he had enough, and he said yes, he was ready to drop. And so we left the sheriff and posse at this point.

(A paragraph of the story is omitted here as the contents have nothing to do with the bank robbery.)

Rising late next morning, we had a leisurely breakfast and drove down to the bank to see what was doing, but right at that moment we knew more than anyone in Rupert did, but not for long. Soon in drove a truck with the sheriff in the seat with the driver, a man or two in the truck body with the dog man and the two big dogs lying on a bed of sacks.

The sheriff was half smiling as he stepped out of the truck, and actually did not look as tired as he had the evening before when he arrived at Rupert. "Did you get them?" was the question on all lips.

"No," he said, "but I got one of their caps." He took out of his overall bib a gray cap, which he said one of them had run out from under when they were fired at. The story was that, soon after we left them last night, some of the men in the posse from Rupert area had called a halt, and asked to talk the situation over. It seemed that they well remembered the old lantern man's theory of the evening before, and they had thought most of the night we were following the X boys just as had been predicted.

Now the dogs apparently were leading straight to the home of the suspected men. A new system should be used, they suggested. The posse should be divided, with the dogs taken from the front and led by the rear contingent, about 200 yards back. All lights should be put out, now unneeded in the bright moonlight. About 8 or 10 men should take the lead with the sheriff, guided by a local man who knew the path to the suspects' houses. All conversation should stop, and the advance party should go forward with all speed possible. The rear party would quickly advance when called.

The sheriff said he took their advice and adopted their plan, and the advance continued. Soon they were about a mile from the objective, and soon the advance party which he was in came out of the woods into a bright moonlit field, and strolling along slowly in the middle of the field toward the houses were the three men about 100 yards away.

One of the posse sprang forward shouting, "Halt, surrender." The sheriff said the three started running like rabbits down the hill, in three different directions. The posse fired numerous shots, but no one was hit. When the sheriff got up to where the criminals had jumped, he picked up the cap. The rear party, hearing the shots, ran up to join the rest. The problem now was that there were three different tracks, and only two dogs to follow them. The sheriff quickly decided which two to follow and they set out to follow again with the dogs leading eagerly.

About daylight the two tracks joined and two posses were one again. At this time the two dogs, after pulling manfully on two men all night, and covering some 15 to 18 miles, gave out and lay down exhausted. This posed a hard problem.

The dog man said, "We will have to carry these dogs out, and I want to get some warm food for them as soon as possible."

A local man came to the rescue. He said the road was about a mile away. "You carry the dogs out there, while I make a bee line for a friend's house about two miles or so away. He has a truck, and I will get him and meet you at the road."

This was done at great labor. Carrying the two big dogs was most exhausting, and the only salvation was that there were several men to share the task. The local man met them with the truck, took them to his house where his wife had breakfast ready for all, including the dogs. The sheriff said he never enjoyed a breakfast so much in his life. He had not stopped at home for supper before starting out last evening and was really hungry.

"Where are the robbers now," we wanted to know.

The sheriff said, "They are in that mountain over there somewhere. I have men posted around it and they may be caught when they come out. One of my deputies is here now in charge. We will watch the railroad stations and notify neighboring authorities. I feel they are fellows who have never been anywhere but here, and know no other life, and even if they make it out of the county, as soon as their money is spent they will come slipping back and be picked up. Now us and the dogs are going home and get some rest."

Thanking all for their help, they transferred to their own car parked beside the bank and departed.

It ended exactly as Sheriff McClung had predicted. The fugitives did get away, and were picked up separately, two of them within a short while, and about six months later the "Charleston Gazette" had a headline, "Last Rupert Bank Robbers Caught."

The Murder Of Zona Heaster

I grew up about fifteen miles from Rainelle, W. Va., the site of possibly the most noted ghost story in the United States. The story concerned the murder of Zona (Heaster) Shue in Greenbrier County and the conviction of her husband, Edward Shue, of her murder due to the evidence presented by her mother who had had visits from the grave by her murdered daughter.

Zona Heaster was a young, beautiful girl when she married Edward Shue, and she died mysteriously two months after that marriage. Zona's mother, Mary Heaster, suspected that her daughter's death was not a natural one, and her suspicions were based on three things: first, the bad reputation of the husband; second, his two previous wives had died violent deaths by strange accidents; third, he had served time in prison for stealing a horse.

Mary Heaster began to pray that her daughter would appear to her and tell her the true story of her death. After a period of time Mary related to those about her that the daughter had indeed appeared at her bedside four times and had told her that her husband had come home from work as a blacksmith, and, in a fit of rage, had broken her neck with his strong blacksmith hands.

Mary Heaster convinced her brother-in-law to help her demand an autopsy. They went to the sheriff of Greenbrier County, who although skeptical, was finally persuaded to order the grave opened and an autopsy performed, going by the minute details provided by the mother, details which she said she had been given by her daughter who had returned from her grave to talk with her. These were details she could not have known firsthand.

The autopsy showed that Zona Heaster Shue's neck was indeed broken as described. The story spread like wildfire! The deaths of Shue's two previous wives came out. Edward Shue was arrested and tried, and the testimony of Mary Heaster was allowed in court by the defense lawyer because he thought it would be treated as ridiculous. However, her testimony, along with the wealth of circumstantial evidence, was convincing, and Edward Shue was sentenced to prison for life, where he died eight years later.

Mary Heaster's daughter now lies in her grave in the cemetery of Soule Chapel Church in a peaceful, rural area of Greenbrier County, and above her grave now stands a monument which reads:

In Memory of Zona Heaster Shue
Greenbrier Ghost
1876-1897

The same brick courthouse where Edward Shue stood trial for murder is standing today, and the records of the murder trial are still there. The words of "The Greenbrier Ghost" are recorded through the testimony of her mother, Mary Heaster.

Did these words actually come from beyond the grave? Twelve serious, solid citizens, after much deliberation, decided that they did. With this decision came the legend of "The Greenbrier Ghost," possibly the most notable ghost story that has persisted through the years in the United States. According to *Case's Comment,* a national lawyers' magazine, this is the only case in the United States where a man has been convicted of murder on the testimony of a ghost.

The Unlawful Baptism Of Edward Shue

As Told By G. S. McKeever

Some weeks ago I read in the Greenbrier Independent, a complete account of the trial and conviction of Edward S. Shue for the murder of his wife near Lewisburg in 1896. Having had some previous experience with Shue, I have been requested by the editor of that paper and a number of other people to write it for publication. However, before giving my own personal experience, I will preface it by relating the following experience of the Reverend R. R. Little, a Methodist preacher, then in charge of a circuit composed of a number of appointments in Greenbrier and Pocahontas Counties. Reverend Little's story as related to me in person at the time of the Shue trial in Lewisburg, is as follows:

"I was called to the Shue home on top of Droop Mountain to perform a marriage ceremony. I arrived there some time in the afternoon of the day appointed for the wedding. The bride-to-be, a mere slip of a girl, was at the Shue home but Edward S. (Trout) Shue had gone for the marriage license. I waited there patiently until far into the night. An atmosphere of tension or uneasiness seemed to embrace all of those present and would not let go. Around midnight Shue came with the license. Preparations were made for a marriage ceremony. The license was passed to me. On examination I found the license was issued in Greenbrier County and the Shue home being in Pocahontas County, I told the contracting parties I could not perform a marriage ceremony in Pocahontas County on a license issued in Greenbrier."

"Shue soon reminded me that it was a moonlight night and that less than a mile would put us across the county line into Greenbrier. So the bride and groom to be, the wedding guests and I proceeded down the country road until we crossed into Greenbrier County to the Schusler place, on the side of Droop Mountain, where I arranged to perform the marriage. When I came to the part of the ceremony where it says, 'If any one has any objections, speak now or forever hold your peace,' I waited, and after some time I said 'I object.' Shue at once demanded to know why I objected. I told him for the reason that the girl he wished to marry was a mere child. None of her people are present. It is now one o'clock in the morning and we are all here in the county road. A marriage ceremony is a sacred rite and should at least be performed under ordinary circumstances. I cannot help but think there is something not right in this case and I will go no farther. So there will be no wedding so far as I am concerned."

"I later understood that the girl was only fifteen years old, that Shue had persuaded her to visit her uncle on Droop Mountain and when he got her away from her parents, had prevailed upon her to marry him, and that they were married in Frankfort the next morning after I had refused to perform the ceremony."

During the year 1886-87, M. W. Walton taught school at Leonard, at Spring Creek. In addition to those people who rightly belonged to this school, there were about eighteen lads from the surrounding community also attending the school. At this time, Shue and his first wife were living in a cabin on Rock Camp Run, a tributary of Spring Creek, and on land belonging to Jim Cutlip, his first wife's father.

Shue was a young man of rather fine physique, apparently of great strength. He had a good singing voice and seemed to take a great delight in singing sacred music. I do not know whether he was connected with any branch of the Christian church. He was a great boaster of his strength; in fact, playing the role of a bully whenever you saw him. Every few days the news could be circulated in the community that Shue had whipped his wife again. This went on for some time. I do not recall who first suggested it, but it was agreed upon among us that we would go to his house some night and give him an ice cold bath in a deep hole of water a short distance from his house.

The mob that gathered was made up of W. M. Walton, the teacher; Jim Walton, Doc Brown, Amos Williams, Jack Hannah, Doak B. Rapp and several others and myself. In casting lots, it fell on Doak Rapp, Jack Hannah and myself to do the bathing. Doak volunteered to call Shue to the door and catch him.

There are some moments that live in your mind forever and this was such a moment. There was the deathlike silence of the winter night and the biting, stinging, frost laden air in our faces. The snow creaked and crumbled under our feet as we silently approached Shue's cabin.

When we reached the cabin, Hannah and I concealed ourselves behind a rock bench just in front of the porch, and Doak stopped at the edge of the porch and called out. Shue came to the door in his night clothes, consisting of a shirt.

Doak asked, "Can you show me the way to Nathan McMillan's?"

Shue replied with the question, "What is your name?"
Doak: "My name is Raymond."
Shue: "Where do you live?"
Doak: "I live near Alderson."
Shue: "I believe I know you."

All this time Doak had been working a little closer to Shue and finally jumped in and caught Shue around the waist. Hannah and I went to Doak's aid and pounced on Shue like wildcats on a rabbit, but before we got there, Shue had succeeded in pulling Doak into the house and had a firm grip on the door facing with his left hand. Hannah and I seized him and the three of us gave a surge. The door facing flew off and Shue fell into our arms as limp as a rag. He never made another struggle but begged for mercy like a child.

We took him down to the water hole, broke through the ice and soused him. Then we told him why we did it. The other members of the mob stood by, not far away, and looked on.

The next day Shue went before Squire Scott at Rennick Valley and swore out a warrant for Doak, Brown, Hannah and myself. Hannah decided to change his boarding place. The warrant was placed in the hands of constable Billy Mike Gillian, who served it on Brown and me. When the state had presented its case, Brown took the stand and testified he was not on Jim Cutlip's place that night and proved it by three of the mob. These statements were all true but they were not called upon to state how close to the Cutlip place they had been. Brown was released by the court, and on a motion made by M. W. Walton, the warrants were set saide.

After this trial Shue's young wife went back to her father's home. Soon after this Shue was sentenced by the Pocahontas Court to the Penitentiary for stealing a horse. While he was in the pen his wife got a divorce and prepared herself as a teacher and taught until she married Tinker McMillan. They reared a large family of intelligent boys and girls.

When Shue returned from prison, it was not long until he married again and set up housekeeping on the top of Droop Mountain where his third wife died under peculiar and suspicious circumstances. He then married the woman for whose murder he was tried and convicted by the circuit court at Lewisburg.

This is a somewhat extended history of possibly one of the greatest criminals of this state. If there ever was such a thing as honor connected with this Shue affair, it was due to my friend, Doak D. Rapp. It was he alone of all those gallant knights, who had the courage to beard the lion in his den. Well, all this happened fifty-six years ago. Mr. Rapp has proved himself an honorable and upright citizen, and I see by the paper that he is aspiring to represent Greenbrier County in the West Virginia House of Delegates.

The only consolation the writer has ever had for participating in the bathing of Shue is that he has felt for a long, long time that the three school boys, totally ignorant of the fact that they were violating the law, took Trout Shue from his home one winter night when the thermometer was registering ten degrees below zero, broke the ice and performed the rites of baptism, without having been first ordained, by emersing him in a deep hole of water, prolonged a good woman's life for many years.

Mediums

Other fascinating stories I used to hear concerned people who consulted mediums to communicate with dead friends or relatives. The most famous of the West Virginia mediums was Amanda Blake, who grew up in Guyandotte, W. Va., now a part of Huntington, W. Va. After marriage she moved to Braddick, Ohio, and spent the remainder of her life as a farm wife and medium.

For forty-five years she conducted seances for 150,000 people, among them politicians and prominent people in all professions and walks of life. One year 300 ministers visited her. Many of the visitors were skeptics and trained investigators whose profession was to expose the hundreds of fake mediums who plied their trade. Many books were written about the investigations, but no fakery was ever proved about Mrs. Blake.

One of Mrs. Blake's visitors was my Aunt Rosa, who wanted to talk with a close friend who had died. When she walked into the room, Mrs. Blake said, "why are you calling on me? You have the gift too, the same as I have." Aunt Rosa thereupon bought the necessary equipment, including the horn, and it worked. People from all over Nicholas County began to call on her to talk with their deceased friends and relatives. Aunt Rosa had no children, and she used to "borrow" one of us for weeks at a time, including me. I later stayed with her when I went to high school. I remember her Ouija Board, which I tried to use, but it failed to answer my questions and I was discouraged — or maybe I got good answers and just wasn't able to spell to receive the answers.

My wife asked Aunt Rosa why she abandoned the practice of a medium, and her reply was that when she entered the room where the horn was kept, it seemed that many spirits were urging her to talk. Since Aunt Rosa was very religious (as was Mrs. Blake), she believed these were evil spirits, and therefore threw the horn away.

My wife still regrets she didn't inherit the horn as a keepsake, as it would have made a great conversation piece.

Another story concerning a medium still being circulated in our county was that of a murder committed about seventy years ago and never solved. Cavendish, "Dish" O'Dell, in his 90's, still living at Quinwood, W. Va., as a young man in his 20's, was given money for expenses to go for a seance with Mrs. Blake. According to his story, the murdered man was contacted and told where he had been, how he had ridden his horse to a certain spot and dismounted. When questioned he would repeat the story of his ride and dismounting, and then he would stop. Each time he was questioned only this part would be repeated. "Dish" O'Dell now refuses to repeat the story, saying it should be forgotten.

There is another experience relating to Mrs. Blake which has been told by a brother and sister I have known since childhood. They believed in mediums. One day they were working in a field on the farm with their father. They stopped working early to go to see Mrs. Blake, leaving their father at work in the field. After driving to Huntington and across the Ohio River, they asked Mrs. Blake to make a contact for them. A voice answered, saying that this was their father, and that he had dropped dead in the field soon after they left him.

I can just imagine the excitement, consternation and disbelief among these early mountain residents of the unexplainable and unknown which happened to them in their day.

Having grown up in that era of ghost stories, they are still of great interest to me today.

An Addition About My Father

In *Mountain Memories II* I have a chapter about my father, Watson Deitz. Since the book has been read by a number of people, both in the family and others, I have found a version of a couple of stories I had never heard, so I will include the new versions in this book.

The first one concerns the incident of the kitchen stove blowing up. It was written by Opal Haynes Anderson in her column, *A Woman's Point Of View,* for the Meadow River Post of Rainelle, W. Va. Her column follows:

One of the nicest things I have been presented with in a long time was a copy of *Mountain Memories II,* written by Dennis Deitz of Charleston, who was born and raised on a Greenbrier County farm not more than two miles from the farm where I was born and raised.

Although Dennis grew up a generation ahead of me, I remember and knew most of the persons he wrote about, and the stories about farm chores and farm living take me back in memory to the farm on Hickory Flat where he grew to adulthood.

We both attended one-room schools, not the same schools or at the same time, but one-room country schools were much alike and provided an education not to be obtained anywhere else.

Dennis was graduated from Rainelle High School in 1932 and as he says, "We grew up in the heart of Appalachia and graduated in the midst of the Great Depression. At the time, our middle class working parents were at the nadir of their economic fortunes or misfortunes. I doubt their average income exceeded $500 per year."

We regret not having known Dennis's dad, Watson Deitz, but always felt we really knew him well as all four of my older brothers and sisters held him in the highest regard. They all had Mr. Deitz for a teacher. In fact the last day he taught before he died was at the school on my grandfather's farm where my brothers and sisters attended classes.

His mother we knew; she also taught school and lived 100

years, and was a very elect lady.

The story Dennis included about the time the hot water tank blew up was a favorite of mine. Seems the water line from the tank to the cook stove froze one cold night and when Watson built a fire the next morning the steam built up in the liner and blew out the end of the cook stove. To add a bit to Dennis's story, "The way I heard it was" his Dad was blown into the pantry through a curtain which covered the door. Hearing the explosion Mrs. Deitz came into the kitchen to investigate. Seeing steam and not her husband, she inquired, "Watson, Watson, where are you?" to which he replied, "In h--- Betty, in h---."

We hope Dennis enjoys this version as much as we children enjoyed having it told to us. Fact or fiction we always thought it was a funny story.

Life was rugged on a mountain farm and the daily chores seemed endless. We girls worked in the fields right along with the boys and enjoyed the air and sunshine. We also did most of the milking, churning and printing butter, picked berries, cherries, pears, plums and apples in season to say nothing about helping in the kitchen and with other housework.

Jalamap Publications, Inc., of Charleston did the printing and we feel you would very much enjoy having a copy of this fast reading book of stories of Dennis's youth and recollections of times past. His stories preserve the past for a rapidly changing society and aid in leading us down a path to our nostalgia childhood of yesteryear.

The other story concerns the time my father was laying up the sleet-covered rail fence which had blown over. I told of the time when several panels of sleet-covered rails had blown down, and my father made several attempts to re-lay the panels. Each time before he quite succeeded the slick, ice covered rails were blown down by the high wind. Finally, when the last rail was in place, he looked heavenward and said, "Now let's see who is the best man." My brother Lawrence tells me there was more to the story as he witnessed the incident. Just after Dad made this statement a great gust of wind again hit the fence, and again the fence went sliding over the hill, leaving Dad under some of the rails and flat on his back. Dad then said, "Lord, can't you take a joke?"

When I wrote the chapter about my father I was limited in my views as I was just fourteen when he died and only had him for a teacher one year. None of his grandchildren remembered him, so I could not get a chapter from a grandchild's point of view. I did have a schoolmate who had gone to school much more than I had and throughout her life often spoke of him. I asked her to write about the things she had often told me, but she was reluctant to do so as she had no confidence in her ability to write. She had gone through only the eighth grade due to the early death of her mother and also economic reasons. She was worried about her grammar, spelling and punctuation.

Finally she agreed to write about him, saying that her daughter would rewrite it and make corrections. I received it too late to put it in *Mountain Memories II*. After reading the story I called her daughter to congratulate her for her gift with words. The daughter said, Oh, no. I typed it, but I didn't have to change three words." Following are the remembrances of Garnet James Bragg about her teacher, who was so sure that she did not have the education or the ability to tell her story.

School Memories

I guess fall is my favorite time of the year. As a child I loved the clear, crisp days and seeing God's handiwork in the brilliantly colored leaves. I loved seeing my breath in the frosty air and finding the chestnuts that snuggled under their blanket of leaves. We children were usually still going barefooted at that time and it was really a thrill to scuff our feet along and uncover those flat brown chestnuts. The only drawback was that we spent many a time picking the chestnut burrs out of our feet!

Fall meant going back to school and I looked forward to that time with much joy and anticipation. Since our nearest neighbor might be several miles away, the only playmates I had were family members. So I was ready to go back to school and be with all of my school pals and our friend and teacher. In my earlier years, our teacher was Mr. Watson Deitz, who taught all the grades in our one-room country school. The schoolhouse was situated on a hill away from all the neighbors, with big rolling fields on one side. We children spent many happy hours running and playing in those fields. In summer most of our time was spent playing "base," but when the snow came, we used these same fields to play "fox and the goose." Mr. Deitz always encouraged us to play outside and get plenty of exercise, but when recess or the noon hour was over, it meant getting back to the business of work.

I've often wondered how Mr. Deitz coped with all of us — children who ranged from six years old to teenage. Our school ran from the first through the eighth grades and Mr. Deitz taught all of us. I know now that he deserved a medal for his patience. But that patience could sometimes be short-fused. Mr. Deitz was a very kind and understanding person for the most part, but when his patience was taxed to the limit, he could be a most explosive man. I know the schoolhouse rafters shuddered many a time when one of us crossed that fine line and drew his wrath.

Mr. Deitz was a man of slight, unimposing build with clear blue eyes and great bushy eyebrows — eyebrows that could be quickly drawn down over eyes that seemed to bore a hole right through a person. Often his glasses would slip down on his nose and he would peer at us over the rims; we were positive he would read our minds.

Mr. Deitz was a wonderful teacher, one who could make our lessons real-life and enjoyable. I especially loved geography and remember vividly how he was able to take me, in my mind, to all of those far-a-way places to meet all the different people.

Many Friday evenings at school were times for a spelling bee. We would divide into two groups and line up on either side of the schoolroom. The competition would run on and on until one person was declared the winner. We also had geography races, where Mr. Deitz would select a city and we would try to locate it on the map, really striving to outdo the other side. It was a challenge to us and school was made so interesting that I looked forward to each new day.

Most of the children lived quite some distance from school and, in those days, no school buses arrived at our doorstep to pick up or deliver us. We walked to and from the schoolhouse each day, a distance of several miles, and I believe my family and I had farther to walk than most of the other students. My brother, two cousins and I made the daily trek through all kinds of weather. Early summer was most fun but we always ran the risk of being late because of dallying to smell a flower, catch a frog, or study any of the other wonderful miracles of nature. In winter the snow would sometimes get so deep that we would make our way through snowdrifts several feet deep. We often arrived cold, and shivering, and we would have to steam ourselves dry around the big Burnside stove that heated the one-room school.

Since I was the only girl in our group, I think Mr. Deitz took pity on me for many times he took me home to spend the night. Mr. Deitz had farther to travel than any of us so he always rode a horse to school. The horse, a big, beautiful chestnut, spent its day in a building next to our schoolhouse where a place had been made for it amid the coal and kindling used to feed our stove. I remember many evenings climbing up behind Mr. Deitz on that big horse and making our way to his house for the night.

Mrs. Deitz taught at another school about a mile or so down the ridge from their house, so she and the children were usually home in the evenings when Mr. Deitz arrived. On the occasions when I was treated to an overnight stay, a warm welcome and the tantalizing smell of cooking greeted us as we walked through the doorway. I don't think I ever had such a wonderful feeling of being welcome.

The evening meal was spent around a large table in their dining room amid the chatter of all the Deitz children telling their news. After the meal was finished, the dishes washed, and all the chores done, Mr. and Mrs. Deitz would go to the living room where they would sit to read or grade papers. I can remember that Mr. Deitz would always doze off, with glasses slipping slowly down his nose. I held my breath many times, just sure they would slip off, but I guess he knew just how far they would slide.

The Deitz home was a rambling two-story farmhouse and we children would usually dash upstairs to play after the evening work was done. The upstairs had a long, wide hall at the top of the stairwell where we were allowed to play our games. The noise we made, I'm sure, sometimes shook the rafters and I know Mr. and

Mrs. Deitz thought their house was coming down around their heads. But the noise was usually ignored and we spent many wonderful hours at play.

In my later school years I attended the school where Mrs. Deitz taught. Mr. Deitz was teaching a few miles farther down the road.

I can still remember the day when, sitting in class, I looked out the window and saw Mr. Deitz slowly making his way down the country road. He was slumped over in the saddle of his great beautiful horse and I knew by the lines etching his face that he was in great pain. When he drew up to our school building, Mrs. Deitz rushed out to meet him. I knew from her expression when she reentered the classroom that Mr. Deitz was very ill. Little was I to know that this would be the last time I would see my beloved teacher and friend. Mr. Deitz passed away several days later, but he left behind a child who had been impressed with his love for learning and one who forever appreciated his wonderful guidance and teachings.

By Garnet James Bragg

Grandfather's Farm 1920

Watson Deitz And New Prospect School

By Macil Haynes Sparks

Fifteen or twenty children stood around, feeling apprehensive, on the first day of school that September morning fifty-seven years ago. We had arrived early to make a good impression on the new teacher we had heard about but had not seen. Fathers of three of us were trustees of the school and had contracted with Watson Deitz to teach that term, 1925-1926. Our parents had told us that he was a tough taskmaster and strict in discipline, so we expected the worst.

My father said that if any of his four children got a switching at school, we could expect the same when we got home.

The girls started a game of tag, and the boys found a round fence rail and see-sawed on the fence which belonged to my father. The fence separated what we called the school house field from the school yard and kept the livestock off the road.

Soon we heard hoof beats of a horse, and the teacher came down the road. One of the pupils showed him the stable behind the school, and we all rushed to our seats and waited.

After ringing his hand bell, the teacher walked to the front of the school and smiled, so we relaxed a bit. He looked around at us, at the oilcloth blackboard, the newly oiled floor that settled the dust, the cold pot-belly stove, the water cooler in the corner, and the lard bucket lunch pails hanging on pegs.

Mr. Deitz told us that the students who finished their work first each day were to be honored by getting to take the water bucket to the neighbor's spring to be filled.

There were only two rows of seats, one on each side of the stove, but each seat was wide enough for two pupils. My brother Cecil and I were in the sixth grade, and we sat together, but he wasn't happy about that arrangement. I was rather messy with my side of the book and paper storage shelf. Our brother Basil and sister Hazel sat together in a smaller seat toward the front. They were in the third grade.

Soon we were settled into our studies and found that dreaded teacher to be kind and helpful. He kept us busy marching up and back to the recitation bench to see how well we had studied our lessons. Not every grade had students, and some had only one or two, but each subject was covered. Stress was made on spelling, reading and arithmetic. Today's subjects are quite different in many categories and were not even thought of in our school. We had penmanship, but art, music and sex education were unheard of.

I remember Watson Deitz as a rather thin man who always wore a suit and vest, and a gold watch chain dangled across his chest. He had graying, sandy hair and spoke with a soft voice. He gave his total attention to all situations.

Mr. Deitz rode a horse or walked over two miles each way to school. Sometimes one of his sons would accompany him and take the horse home to work on the farm.

It is not surprising that, being human, he got tired and stretched out on the recitation bench to relax after eating lunch, while the kids raced outside to play base or tag, or one of the many games we played. On nice days someone would sneak in to see if he were still sleeping. If so, the whole school would head for the school house field and play a game of run-sheep-run that could take us out of hearing. We hoped Mr. Deitz would snooze past the lunch hour. One little boy was the only first grader and couldn't keep up, so he would go back and wake the teacher. A couple of us would boost the little boy up on a rock cliff that he dared not descend by himself, and we would leave him there until the game was over.

One time Mr. Deitz surprised us and went to the field, where he found the boy marooned on the rock. After school Glenna Nutter and I were detained a minute and the teacher asked us to watch the little boy who had somehow mysteriously climbed a rock and couldn't get down. He asked us to be on guard to see that it didn't happen again.

Mr. Deitz spent a lot of time preparing for a visit from the Greenbrier County Superintendent of Schools, who made an unscheduled yearly visit, such as a surprise visit by a bank examiner scares bank tellers. We were told in advance that we would study a certain lesson in reading and spelling so we would know every word. Finally we saw a tall, severe looking man passing the big oak tree as we played at recess. When the bell rang, and all were in their seats, the Superintendent sat in the back of the room and listened as each class was called to the recitation bench. Everybody read and spelled to perfection. This preparation for the Superintendent was practiced by all our teachers.

Across the road in the woods there were many wild grape vines growing, with the vines reaching high up in the trees. One of the older boys would chop the vine off at the ground, and we would soar on the swing for a season. When the vines would die and fall. We would then get another vine.

The school house field was a good place to sleigh ride in winter on our home-made sleds. The grounds surrounding the school house were a muddy mess after the snow started, except when it was frozen so we could run and play. We always played in the road, for traffic was rare, and then there was only a horse or someone walking. Perhaps a wagon or car came along once a month.

When frost and snow came, the children put on their shoes, long underwear and heavy clothes. Most of our shoes had high tops, and we wore galoshes over them. We would spend a few minutes every morning warming our toes around the stove, which the student-janitor had fired up early with kindling and coal. The stove was segmented, with a base which held the grate and a drawer to catch the ashes. The bottom section was joined to a fat bowl that gave it the name of pot-belly. There was a door in that section. On top was an inverted bowl with a collar that supported the long pipe which went through the ceiling.

The red hot and cooling periods of the cast iron eventually cracked some part of the metal, and it was an annual event when the stove broke apart and fell, scattering coals and ashes over the wood floor. A fast scramble took the students outside, while the teacher and older pupils cleaned up the mess.

One of the trustees was hastily notified to buy a new section for the stove at the local country store at Russellville, where almost everything could be bought. (The storekeeper also traded goods for our eggs and butter.)

I haven't really said as much about Watson Deitz as about the life and times of New Prospect School as I remember them when I was twelve years old and in the sixth grade. I do remember well the day after Halloween when a couple of neighbors were sent for to set up the outdoor privies because some "off campus" rowdies had pushed them over the night before. My father, Clarence "Root" Haynes, was the first one summoned, as he was a general handyman and could fix almost anything. I suppose it wasn't much of a job as the little buildings were built open-pit, with no hole under them. Mr. Deitz was pretty mad and swore to find who did such a dastardly deed.

Our spelling books were written to last through grade school, with easy, one syllable words in the front. There was a gradual progression to hard words in the back for the eighth graders. Every Friday afternoon, after recess, it was traditional to have a spelling match, with two leaders appointed to choose sides. They tried to get the best spellers to stand beside them on their side of the room. They spelled down the ones who missed a word until only two were left, or the one with the most marks was declared the winner. Hard words were given to the older students, and the teacher kept his finger in the front of the book to find words for the tots. What a shout would go up when a younger pupil spelled down an eighth grader! My sister, Hazel, frequently did this.

New Prospect School, like many schools in those days, had no library, magazines or newspapers. Most of us had little of this reading material at home, but we had our Bibles and Sunday School literature. We learned a lot by helping our parents, and, without television or radio, we could concentrate on other things around us. We watched the things in nature and the changes in seasons. We knew when chestnuts and other nuts ripened, and we kept busy harvesting them in the woods, where plenty of them grew. Most of the children our age knew about milking cows, caring for farm animals, gardening in summer, raking hay, and doing other, almost endless chores.

Our social life revolved around school and church, plus visiting our neighbors. The lower Hickory Flat was the center of the universe for us, and the rest of the world was a far-a-way place with far-a-way people. It was hard to think of what we read in our geography books in three dimensions. The places were names on maps that we wondered about.

Our neighborhood was first settled by four Haynes brothers, whose parents and grandparents lived on the Fayette County side of Russellville. All of these ancestors are buried in area cemeteries. I have visited many of these graves. Most of the students in New Prospect School were cousins to some degree, with many having the same last name. There was a saying that if a stranger traveling Hickory Flat road met someone and said, "Hello, Mr. Nutter," and got no answer, all he had to say was, "Hello, Mr. Haynes," and he would be right. We lived on land our grandfather cleared and built the first house on, about three-fourths of a mile from the school. We had a rather steep, windy hill to travel through our fields.

My Mother, Dona Haynes, was a midwife and frequently got up in the middle of the night to deliver a baby. Our grandmother was very old-fashioned and told us that babies were found in hollow logs. We believed this until reason took over, and we demanded a better explanation.

Eventually there were seven in our family, with three brothers being deceased now. One brother, Earl, and the three girls are still alive.

Our grandmother, who was also a midwife and delivered many children, often told us that all foolery is sin, and that included cards, dancing and reading novels. Everyone knew her as Aunt Nellie.

I had a hard time learning the multiplication tables, so Mr. Deitz asked me to study them at home, and my father spent many evenings by lamp light helping me memorize those figures. The page got all grimy and tattered from fingering. Our parents bought our books at the general store in Lookout. If our pencils got short too soon and tablets were used up quickly, Dad wondered why. Both sides of all paper were written on, and then it was used to make little drinking cups for water from the cooler. The blackboard was used as often as possible to write lessons. Once, when I was at the board, I made faces behind Mr. Deitz's back so the other kids would laugh. When he caught on to my act, he sharply reprimanded me, and he told me that, since it was winter, my face would freeze in that shape. Then he ordered me to make a face and stand there for a few minutes. Generally Mr. Deitz made me feel I was dong well, and that was very encouraging.

I wish I could remember which neighbor children were there that year, but I do know Joe and Stella Nutter's three children were pupils, and Myrtle Haynes had three in school. There were two Short boys, two of Lonzo Boley's boys, two of Sam Haynes's boys, and a few more I am sure. I hope that those I have forgotten will forgive my short memory.

Mr. Deitz taught at another school the following year, but when I was to be in the eighth grade, he was employed to teach us again, much to our delight, for he was a legend by this time. I am glad to be able to say that all of the teachers we had in grade school were excellent and did their best to teach us what they could, but Mr. Deitz was special to us. We greeted him warmly, but our joy was short lived. He became ill after only a few days and lay down under a large tree on the grass where we pitched horseshoes. We could see he was in great pain, but we were helpless to do anything. At his request, one of the boys walked to the Deitz home to get a member of his family to bring a horse to take him home. With much difficulty and help from the students, he mounted the horse and went up the road, with his son walking beside him. That was the last time we saw him alive, for he died in a few days.

Several of the students walked to the Sugar Grove church for the funeral, a distance of about four miles. The crowd was so large the funeral was held outside under the trees. That was a sad day for the family, his former students and for all who knew him.

About ten years later our family had relatives visiting from out of town, and we took a ride up Hickory Flat road. When we passed the Deitz home, Helen was in the yard, and we stopped to greet her. She asked us in to visit. Some other members of the family were there, and soon they brought out some games which we played. Miraculously a large chocolate cake appeared, and there was a pot of coffee. That was an example of southern hospitality.

In 1980 when I visited West Virginia, my sister Opal and brother-in-law, Ed Anderson, asked where I would like to go, and I said I would like to take a ride from Russellville to Quinwood on a familiar road. Many places I remembered were gone or changed. On the school ground were large trees, and this was true in the yards where friends had once lived. Many places looked the same as when I lived in the area, but most of the people have moved or died. It was a day of bittersweet memories. When we reached Sugar Grove church, I walked through the cemetery, and the first thing I saw was Mr. Deitz's monument. I can't describe my feelings. I looked around and could see many miles in each direction, with the firetower nearby. There were rows of deep green ridges, with fog sandwiched between some of them. It is a beautiful, peaceful spot to rest out eternity.

It was a pleasure knowing Mr. Deitz, and I appreciate his influence on my life.

In Mountain Memories II *I tell of my brother, Granville, as I remember him. Since I never worked with him I had a couple of people who did work with him and a long-time friend who had both worked and fished with him to write about their memories of him. I am including a few of Granville's stories I had not published in* Mountain Memories.

Something About Granville A. Deitz

By R. M. Cottle
Rt. 2, Box 225, Fayetteville, W. Va.

One evening in the late fall of 1950 Granville and A. E. Tross were on their way to the home of one of his insurance agents. A new baby had been born in this home, the sixth in six years. As they turned in at the farm a duck ran across the road, and Tross said to Granville, "What was that?" Granville said that was a stork. Tross said he thought a stork had long legs, and Granville replied, "A stork does have long legs, but that one has worn his legs off bringing babies to this house."

Granville A. Deitz, as he came to be known, was the living epitome of the American dream. He became one of the leading superintendents in the insurance company for which I worked. He was a hard worker, and bad weather or bad roads never kept him from his work. He provided leadership and was sympathetic and kindly with his agents. He was a good and true friend to his company and to the agents who worked for him. His agents were always glad for him to be with them.

Granville A. Deitz was much more than just a successful business and professional man. He was a loving son, brother, father and husband. He regarded his family as the true center of his world. He was devoted to all of them. He adored his daughter and idolized his wife. In return, his family loved and respected him, and his home was a happy place.

I visited in his home a few times, and we had long talks, punctuated with laughter from all who were in his company. In Granville's presence there was light from happy eyes, the warmth of loving hearts, and kindness, loyalty and companionship. He will remain in the hearts of all his friends and family as a precious and everlasting memory.

A Friend

He was my friend, and he was your friend,
He made his friends by being one.
On his friendship man relied
In every deed that needed to be done.
He made the Golden Rule his guide.
His friendly presence brought a cheer
That made the day seem wondrous fair,
His daily living so sincere
He made others love him everywhere.
He was a friend.

The brightness of the day is gone.
We see the setting of the sun!
If only we could carry on
And live a life as he has done.
Just yonder on the star-kissed shore
He carries on a nobler way
Though we can see his face no more.
Thanks for his friendship for a day —
He was a friend.

By R. M. Cottle

Fletcher And Granville

In talking with Fletcher Andrews I tried to get him to record some of his stories and travels with my brother, Granville A. Deitz. Following are some of his experiences and feelings about Granville.

I met Granville in the fall of 1954. I had heard from different sources, especially from my brother who had married Granville's sister, that Granville was an excellent salesman, and my company was looking for good salesmen, so I was eager to meet Granville.

He impressed me with his boundless energy and enthusiasm, and his subtle wit appealed to me. I could see that he was determined to succeed in whatever he attempted.

Dennis mentioned to me when he and his wife were visiting in our home in Elkins that Granville might be interested in changing companies if he could get a favorable situation, so I called Granville and went to St. Albans to meet with him at his home. He decided to come with our company, Mutual of Omaha.

Granville had a unique approach to selling, what we call reverse psychology. He put the prospect into a position where it seemed like the insurance might be a little difficult to buy because the company was very selective in insuring people and wanted only the very best risks possible. This made the prospect have the feeling that Granville was really doing him a favor by even being at his home. He had a unique habit of expressing these ideas very carefully, and often during the interview it seemed as if he were really a very busy person and had to get the application written and get going to meet other prospects.

Granville was one of the best service men with his policy holders that I ever knew. It didn't make any difference what hour of the day or night anyone called him, wanting help with a claim or having a question about the insurance, he went all out to help in every way he possibly could.

Not that Granville meant to be funny or humorous, but he would say things that really struck my funnybone. For instance,

Granville had an office in Parkersburg, and I visited him there quite often. I hired new agents for the company, and then Granville would work with them from time to time. We hired one fellow who seemed like he was going to be a really great salesman. He just seemed to work hard, and he sold a lot of insurance. After three or four months he seemed to quit working very much, and some of the insurance he did sell was rather questionable. I mentioned this to Granville and said I didn't know whether or not the man was going to work out satisfactorily, for he didn't seem to be measuring up to what we expected of him. Granville said, "Oh, yeah, that's right, Andy. You really got to know him not to like him."

On another occasion I was working with Granville, and we went to call on a lady who had written that she was interested in getting a hospitalization plan. Granville carefully explained the insurance to her, and after spending about two hours, the lady bought three policies.

She mentioned before we left that we certainly were different from most insurance men who had ever called on her, for we didn't use any high pressure and didn't try to force her to buy anything. Granville said, "Mrs. Smith, we would never do anything like that. We are just happy to come to your home and explain the policy to you, take your application and send it in to the company. We're just glad to do that. Of course, if you didn't want to buy the insurance, we'd just burn your house and leave."

One time when the company had given us a trip to the beach Granville and I went to a very exclusive club called the Vagabon for dinner. They had French waiters, and I think they were from Jamaica, or somewhere in the Carribean. When the waiter came around to Granville to take his order, Granville had a puzzled look on his face, and he said, "Do you know my favorite dish just isn't on this menu." In his broken English the waiter wanted to know what it was. Granville said, "Well, I was just hoping to have scrambled elephant brains and applebutter."

Another time when Granville had been calling on a lady prospect I asked him when he got back if he had sold the lady the policy. He said she had a policy with White Cross Insurance Company and just wanted to compare Mutual of Omaha with the White Cross plan, and I said, "Well, did you compare!" He said, "Well, yes, I did. I thought I did a wonderful job of comparing them. I told her that to compare the great and wonderful and glorious Mutual of Omaha with the White Cross was like comparing the brilliant rays of midday sun with a black suit and a black cat's butt at midnight in a London fog." He said, "Now I thought that was a fair comparison don't you?"

Granville was possibly one of the most impatient fellows I have ever known. He had a rather short fuse. I recall we were going through Weirton one evening just when the shifts were changing at the mill, and we were only able to move about four or five feet and then wait and wait to move another four or five feet. Granville became more and more impatient. He finally said, "Andy, this sort of thing makes me want to resign from the human race."

Another time I went with Granville to the Chancellor Cafeteria in Parkersburg. He had been wanting to go there to get a steak because he said they had the best steaks of any place he knew of. He insisted that he was going to take me to the Chancellor and buy me a porterhouse steak. I am of the Catholic faith, and at that time Catholics weren't supposed to eat meat on Friday, and this was Friday. After we sat down it occurred to me that this was Friday, and I said, "Gee whiz, Granville, this is Friday, and I can't have meat on Friday." He said, "Well, I just wish you could have one of these steaks this evening. I'll tell you what I'm going to do. I'm going to order one for myself, and I'm going to dedicate it to you."

Granville used to introduce me every now and then to someone and say, "Now, Andy's not nearly as nice a fellow as I am, but he is way above average."

Another time when Granville was impatient with traffic he said, "Dang it, Andy, I'd go to outer space if it weren't for this dang traffic."

Granville had no religious prejudice whatsoever that I've ever known about. One time he told me a story about stopping at a little store in Greenbrier County, and the lady who ran the store and two or three other ladies were discussing religion. He stood around and listened to them for a little while, and one of the ladies said, "Another thing about those Catholics, you know, is they believe they can pray someone right out of hell." Granville said, "Now, ladies, I don't want to butt in here or anything, but I do want to say this. Now, there was a very good friend of mine who was a Catholic, and he died and was going right into hell, and they prayed him out of there, but I tell you his right leg was scorched to beat the devil."

Another time Granville and I were discussing a mutual acquaintance of ours. It seemed like these folks were always wanting to borrow money or were always running up big charge accounts. Granville made the remark that they'd buy hell if they could buy it on credit.

Granville's wife, Peg, always had a whistling tea kettle — one of those tea kettles that whistle when the water gets hot. Their daughter came into the house one day, and the kettle was whistling. She said, "Daddy, why is she having that tea kettle whistle like that all the time?" Granville said, "Oh, I think she's trying to make holy water, so she's just boiling the hell out of it."

A Story About Granville Deitz

By Edgar Buster

As Told To Dennis Deitz

Edgar always considered it one of the luckiest days in his life when Dennis, Granville's brother, introduced him to Granville, whom he came to love and respect very much. He said Granville was a generous person, but he also had a little, short fuse. He could fly off the handle easy and fly back on just as quickly.

According to Edgar, "Granville and I spent a lot of good times together hunting, fishing, talking and playing cards. He had a lot of dry humor. I knew that when he didn't like anything he would say, 'Well, I hate that as much as the devil hates holy water.' "

Granville loved catfish dinners, and every year he and I'd go fishing, I think for 14 straight years. We spent a week fishing each winter. Granville would always insist on going to this restaurant where they specialized in catfish, and we went there at least two or three times while we were down there.

One time when we were coming back from Florida, Granville got on an interchange at Monroe, South Carolina. It was either South or North Carolina, I'm not sure. But, anyway, he made about five or six circles around the thing, trying to get off of it. He said there was no way in God's world to get off of one of those things when you get on it.

Another time when we were going to Florida to fish, Granville was driving my car, and I was settin' there half alseep. I'd wake up and say, "Granville how's the gas situation?" He'd say, "We got half a tank." We went on an hour or two more, and I asked about the gas situation. He said, "Oh, we're doing fine. Got about half a tank." About fifteen or twenty minutes later we ran out of gas. I said, "Granville, what were you looking at?" He was looking at the generator charge thing instead of the gas gauge. He said the gas gauge was in that place on his car. We were lucky enough to be almost to a filling station when we ran out.

Granville loved to play poker, and he was a good poker player, but there was one of the guys who played with us that Granville loved to get his goat and get him mad. Well, it'd be about half way through a hand, and Granville would look up at this guy and say, "Now, let me get this straight. Does three of a kind beat a two pair?" Barry would say, "Granville, you know good and well that three of a kind beats two pair. What are you trying to pull?" Granville would say, "That's right, it does. Now a straight will beat a flush, won't it?" Barry would go into another fit and tell him he knew better than that. But, anyway, he'd end up having Barry real upset, which didn't help him any in a poker game.

Granville and I used to go down to Tennessee and fish quite a bit. We'd get us a map, and we'd look at how to get down there. Just before the end of the Turnpike we'd try to figure out short cuts. He and I were both alike, and we'd try to figure out how to see new territory, and some days we'd get up into the mountains on trails you wouldn't believe. We were lost about three or four hours one time. When we came back Granville was telling everyone he saw that we lost a lot of time, but we saw a lot of new territory, and we freed some slaves; that we ran into one old mountaineer up there who still had his slaves and didn't know they'd been set free.

I always considered Granville one of my best friends, if not the best. I loved him. He was a warm hearted person who would do anything he could for anybody if he could.

He was just a real good story teller, which I'm not. He could tell you the same story three or four times, and you'd still be interested in it. He just had a knack for that sort of thing. I spent a lot of good times with Granville, and I sure have missed him. I guess that Granville was one of the best insurance salesmen. I know lots of times we'd be riding along, and both of us would be kind of drowsy, and Granville would start making up his speech to sell somebody insurance. I'd sit there and listen to him.

The first time we went to Lake Okeechobee on a fishing trip we hired an Indian guide who showed us where to fish and how to fish. Of course, he took us eight or ten miles out of the way to get there, hoping we couldn't find it ourselves, but we always got back. Anyway, that day Granville and I had gone down there, and we just had tackle we used around West Virginia and Tennessee, Zebco reels and six and eight pound test line. Those fish would take all the line we had. We didn't have a bit left when the day was over, so that night we went into Moorehaven, and Granville bought a real expensive rod and reel, a heavy one. I wasn't as well off as Granville, so I just bought heavy lines and was gonna make do with what I had. The next day we went out and starting fishing. After we fished a little while, I saw Granville sit down. I was running the boat in the back end, and he was up front on the seat. He sat there, and he worked and worked, and I watched him. I thought it's about time for him to blow up, so I stood up. About that time he jumped up and took that new rod and reel and was going to throw it right in the middle of the lake. I reached up and took it out of his hand. I never will forget that. I sat down with it for five minutes and got it untangled for him and gave it back to him. He would fly off the handle real quick, and then he'd fly right back on, but I never saw him mad at anybody — only himself. He was just that kind of a person. I have to say that I enjoyed his company and enjoyed fishing and hunting with him more than anyone I ever hunted or fished with, and I just wish we could still do it.

Granville was very civic minded and took a lot of pride in politics. He told me that he always voted for the best man, and the way he knew he was the best man was because he was a Republican.

Our Neighbor

We were reasonably close neighbors to a farmer, who like all rugged individualists of that day and time, was a character who stood out even in that neighborhood of individual characters. That was one thing about the community in which I was born: there were no conformists.

This man was pure Irish and, like all Irishmen, was a devoted family man. He was tender hearted to an unusual degree so far as his family was concerned. For the sake of the story, we will call this man Duffy, which is a good Irish name. He had a large family, which he loved above all other things on the good earth, but his oldest son, Jim, was the true apple of his eye. To Jim he attributed all of the qualities of which mankind is blessed. To Jim he attributed the wisdom of Solomon, the strength of Sampson, and the mature judgement of the great Judge Marshall. In a very short time he would be governor of the state, and from there it was only a short step to the presidency. In fact, Duffy thought Jim would be the first Catholic president.

In those days very few of our neighborhood boys managed to get to college, but Duffy sent Jim to the University, and shortly thereafter wondrous news spread throughout the neighborhood, — transmitted by Duffy. Jim was making the best grades at the university. He was the most popular man. The entire city in which the university was located was marveling at this prodigy in their midst. Duffy firmly believed that by Jim's senior year he would hold down two jobs: that of class president and president of the university. At this time disaster struck. We were in the midst of World War I, and Uncle Sam drafted Jim.

To Duffy, this was no draft of an ordinary mortal. Woodrow Wilson, the President, could have been drafted to fight in the ranks, and Duffy would have given it no thought. All of congress could have been called to ranks, and Duffy would have felt that since they declared the war it was strictly okay. The young men of the neighborhood were being drafted, and he felt this was only normal procedure. After all, there was a war to be fought, but for Uncle Sam to draft Jim was the most monstrous thing in the history of mankind. This was a crime against humanity.

Jim came home before going to camp, and, since Duffy did not feel he was in position to take on Uncle Sam in person, he took Jim to the railroad station some 15 miles away to catch a train to Camp Lee, Virginia. They went by horseback as Duffy did not have a car at that time. Jim boarded the train bound for Camp Lee, and Duffy climbed aboard his trusty horse and started that lonesome ride home, leading Jim's horse.

The farther Duffy rode, the madder he became, as he contemplated this great wrong done his son Jim by Uncle Sam in drafting him to fight as a common soldier across the sea. At least he could have started Jim as Commander in Chief, befitting a man of Jim's talents.

The farther Duffy rode the madder he got at the way Jim had been mistreated. When he came to the little lumber town of Nallen, he saw an Italian laborer on the railroad track, working on the track. Duffy rode up to him and said in his fine Irish brogue, "What are you doing over here working at high wages, and my son Jim across the seas, fighting your bloody battles?"

At this time Jim had not yet cleared the West Virginia border on his way to Camp Lee.

The Italian looked at Duffy in bewilderment. About this time the general superintendent of the lumber company came by and, hearing Duffy haranguing the Italian and knowing Duffy well, he asked what the trouble was.

Duffy turned to Mr. Young and said, "And I think but damn little of ye, Mr. Young, working these foreign devils and me poor son Jim across the seas fighting their bloody battles." The Italian looked at Mr. Young and tapped his forehead and said, "Crazy man, Mr. Young, crazy man." This so enraged Duffy that he jumped off his horse and ran the Italian a quarter of a mile down the track trying to catch him to give him a licking. It was lucky for the Italian he managed to out run Duffy.

A few months passed by, and the war ended. Jim was still at Camp Lee and was still a private. Evidently the army did not know a super man when they saw one. In the meantime, Duffy had purchased an automobile. Even in those days, every country family of any means had a country telephone. One night the telephone rang, and Jim's voice came through loud and clear: "Father, I am at Winona, home from the war. Come and get me." Jim answered, "Son, I will be there within an hour." Now, Winona was fifteen miles away through the mountains, and this was just about an hour's drive by car, but it was several hours by horse. Duffy had forgotten that his car, as usual, was broken down. He could not call back to tell Jim that instead of an hour it would be three or four hours. He did not know where Jim had called from, so Duffy got excited and said to his wife, Iris, "Iris, start cooking. Our son Jim is home from the war." To his daughters, he said, "Ethel, kill a chicken. Lucy, bake a cake. Margaret, make a salad." Then he turned to his son, Robert, and said, "Go saddle two horses and be spurring them until I get there." Duffy wanted them well warmed up for a running start.

I am not aware of the final mark in life made by Jim, but I presume that, if he is still living, he is the head of some mighty corporation or at least prominent in some field. I have often wondered if the first computer might not be Jim' brain mechanized.

A Mountain Debate Of About 1914

There were very few amusement centers in Hillbilly land when I was a boy. People went to church because it was a way of life, because it was the spiritual center of the community, and because it was the chief social center.

The next most prominent facet of community life was the school, mostly a one-room school. It was here that were held the box-socials, the cake walks, and the get-togethers that were considered slightly too worldly to be held in the church. It was here that frequently the community would attend a debate, a popular form of entertainment. Usually it was entertaining as well as informative, but, usually, the subject discussed was not of a sophisticated nature, but of a historical or political nature that the audience could appreciate.

The particular incident which I am going to narrate was debated by two men of the community, Mr. A. and Mr. B., and they still have many relatives in the community.

Mr. A was a Republican, whose father had fought with the Union forces in the Civil War, and he ardently believed that Abraham Lincoln was the greatest man who had lived since a man of Galilee.

Mr. B. was a Democrat, whose father had fought with the Confederate forces, and he was definitely not a pro-Lincoln man in any sense of the word.

These men were neighbors and reasonably good friends except for politics and the Civil War. Both were literate men, and often when a case was being tried before a justice of peace, one or sometimes both would be involved as would-be Blackstones, representing the plaintiff or the defendant. They were good country speakers and were capable of using language that would appeal to their audiences.

The subject of this debate was Resolved: that Abraham Lincoln was greater than George Washington. Each was to be allowed the necessary time for his speech, but each was limited to a three minute rebuttal. Mr. A, the proponent of the affirmative, Abraham Lincoln, led off, and here is what he said:

Honorable Judges, Friends and Neighbors: I cannot understand why this subject could possibly be open to debate, nor can I understand how my opponent could be victimized without taking the negative side of this question, a task as hopeless as trying to count the grains of sand at the seashore or the stars in the heavens. The great Lincoln stands all alone in the pages of the history of America. He is a man of the ages, whose like will never be seen again. The mold is broken and he stands immortalized and alone, looking down from above on the great America that he preserved. He was a man of humble origin. Even as the man of Galilee was born of humble parents and in a manger, the great Lincoln was born in poverty in a little log cabin. From the very beginning he started to prepare himself for the role which destiny had chosen for him to play in the history of his country. He studied at night by the glow of the firelight. He had a yearning for knowledge and left no stone unturned in order to educate himself as a lawyer. He split rails, even as you and I. He learned the language of the people, for he was one of them. Their problems were his problems, and their joys were also his. He came up slowly but surely. His life was built on a foundation of honest toil and common sense. Gradually people came to realize that here was an uncommon man from common origin. He was a man of humor and wit, an orator gifted as few orators have been gifted. Thus, when this great civil conflict that turned brother against brother came to pass, luckily the people had chosen as their leader the great Lincoln. He readily saw that the real question was not slavery, but the preservation of our country. To this task he brought his great heart and mind. He freed the slaves, he preserved the union, and if an assassin's bullet had not taken him away, he would have bound up the wounds of the war between the states with a minimum of hate and discord. He is the all-time great of American history, and it seems more than passing strange to me that there should be a comparison of greatness between this great man and George Washington, a man, who under the pretext of surveying, was an opportunistic land grabber, who came over the mountains of western Virginia only to pick out nice tracts of level land for his future needs; a man so stupid he could not tell a lie. As all of you know, Honorable Judges, Friends, and Neighbors, even a child can tell a lie. A man who spent several years running from the British with his men, and won only in the end when they became wearied of conflict so far away from home, and the expense entailed. It is an insult to the memory of the great Lincoln to compare him with this surveying, land-grabbing

Washington. Thank you, and I will now give the floor to my opponent, and the impossible task facing him.

Mr. B took the floor, and this is what he said:

Honorable Judges, Friends, and Neighbors: It is both a pleasure and also an honor to be allowed to pay tribute to the greatest name that has ever been recorded on the history of this continent, and will continue to be so honored so long as there is a record of human deeds and human events.

I feel sure that all of you in this room realize that if it were not for the immortal George Washington, the father of this country, that we very probably would still be part of and paying tribute to a nation across the sea.

Here was a man born to greatness, and from the beginning he was a success. My opponent speaks of him being so stupid that he could not tell a lie. It is true that he could not tell a lie. He was just as incapable of telling a lie as some are incapable of taking God's name in vain. He had such moral and spiritual integrity that a lie was absolutely abhorrent to his nature. He had a quick and a clear mind. He became an expert surveyor at an age when most young men were beginning to learn to till the soil. Along with this intelligence and clear mind, he was the strongest man in that section of his state. He had an arm that was strong enough to have made him the greatest baseball pitcher of his time if baseball had been played in his time. In other words, Honorable Judges and neighbors, here was a man who was the acme of mental and physical perfection. A man of highest moral character. My opponent speaks of this great man as a land grabber. He was commissioned by the Colonial Governor of Virginia to survey and explore this western land that was termed a wilderness, and his only pay was in the form of land grants, as was the custom of the day, and would it not have been strangely stupid if he would have chosen barren hill-side rocky land. He fulfilled the task given him, and to the satisfaction of the authority that sent him, and as they saw the capabilities of this amazing man, more and more responsibilities were thrust upon him. He covered the mistakes of Braddock by saving the army, after Braddock had led it into a trap, and paid for the mistake with his life. When it became clear that these young and vital colonies must separate from the motherland if they were to endure and prosper, there was one man and only one man with the courage, the foresight and the military know how to combat the forces of this mightiest of nations, and also the might of her hired mercenaries. He was the only man even considered for its first president. He was the only man capable of welding together for the common good such rugged individuals as Thomas Jefferson, Alexander Hamilton, and the Adamses of Massachusetts. He could have been president until the day he died, but he wished to set a precedent as a guide line for the future, but during his presidency he set up a stable government. He chose his cabinet wisely and well, and under his presidency our present currency system, which we still use in its original form, was set up.

During his presidency and under his leadership we have our constitution, the greatest and wisest document of government and freedom ever evolved, and when he left office he delivered his farewell address. For wisdom and clarity it can only be compared to the constitution or the Declaration of Independence. He retired to Mount Vernon, and again he showed his countrymen the virtues of rotation of crops, better methods of farming. His illustrious life from the cradle to the grave is written in gold on the pages of our history. A man who was successful in every endeavor; a man who was a living hero and a legend even among the great men of his time.

It is beyond my understanding how this illustrious warrior and statesman, who was first in war and first in peace and first in the hearts of his countrymen. It is incomprehensible how there should be any manner of comparison with that of Abraham Lincoln; a man that was a failure in every endeavor. Lincoln was a failure in business. As a warrior he went with a little band to fight the Indians, and they disbanded before ever coming to grips with the redskins. He was a henpecked husband and a frustrated character. He became president in a time when there was such confusion and uncertainty that really no one wanted it, and the country was looking for a scape-goat. The war should have been won in a few months, due to the fact that the brave men of the confederate army were outmanned four to one. The manufacturing capacity was in the north. They were blockaded by sea, and it was only through the utterly stupid appointments by Lincoln of the generals to command the Union forces that prolonged the war. Never in history did military might of such overwhelming force perform so little with so much, and finally after four long years the Confederate armies, barefoot, without food or supplies gave up the struggle. The Union was preserved in spite of Mr. Lincoln and his appointments so stupid as to be without parallel in the history of warfare. The choice, Honorable Judges and neighbors, is as clear-cut as success and failure. The successful and heroic Father of Our Country and a henpecked husband. A failure in both peace and war. I thank you.

Mr. A was given the floor for three minutes or less of rebuttal.

Honorable Judges and good neighbors. It was with both amazement and disgust that I listened to my opponent try to make into heroic proportions a land-grabbing surveyor of doubtful ability. It reminded me of someone puffing and panting and getting red-faced trying to blow up a balloon or, as stated in the Holy Writ, of making a mountain out a molehill. I would like to say to you, Honorable Judges and friends, that we are here to judge the merits and the greatness of the statesmanship of two men. I am referring to the Great Lincoln, the noblest American of them all. A man of humble surroundings, who alone and unaided, came to the highest office our country affords. Who preserved this country? Who broke the bonds of slavery for a great race. And who finally died for his country. My opponent pleads for a man who was born with a silver spoon in his mouth. A man who had connections. A man who was an opportunist for personal gain. I leave with you, secure in your good judgment the Immortal Lincoln. Thank you.

Mr. B was given the floor for three minutes or less of rebuttal.
Honorable Judge, Friends and Neighbors. I will make this short and to the point. In the Immortal Washington you are viewing the career of a man great from almost the cradle to the grave. Strong in body and in mind, successful in both war and peace. The father, in fact the very architect of this country in which we live. In Mr. Lincoln we are viewing a long series of failures. He failed in peace. He failed in business. He was a long series of failures in war. He must have been a failure in marriage as he was one of the worst hen-pecked husbands on record.
I say to you to compare the great and noble Washington with that frustrated and failure Lincoln is, even as comparing the brilliant rays of the noon-day sun to the feeble light of a soup bean in a black cat's a-- in a London fog. Thank you.

Unfortunately no judges' decision was ever rendered on this debate. The room was full of neighbors whose fathers had fought in the war between the states, and there was some feeling exposed. Between speeches some of the people had freely indulged in some of Jo Jack's special fighting brew, and within seconds fists were swinging, and a fiddle and a banjo were broken over heads of the combatants before some cooler heads intervened. By the following Sunday all was well, and the usual neighborly spirit had returned. Mr. A invitied Mr. B and his family to Sunday dinner. The invitation was accepted, and peace had returned to the community again, even as it had following the war, but there is still to this day some private discussion and difference of opinion on the respective merits of the two great national figures, and also as to who had the better of the debate, but, as said before, these debates were instructive, edifying and amusing, and sometimes they ended in a fight. We had no movies, but we could always stir up a debate.

Was It A Rat, Or Was It A Mouse?

Mr. and Mrs. Brown lived in our community, and they were numbered among our more substantial citizens. They owned one of the nicer farms and had been married for thirty-eight years. They had five children who turned out well, and who had in turn gotten married and had families of their own. They had always gotten along well, as they were both even tempered, well adjusted people, and their married life had gone along with a minimum of discord.

One night they were sitting before an open wood fire in their living room, occasionally talking, but mostly just watching the logs burn and crackle. Suddenly Mr. Brown raised up in his chair and said, "Mary, did you see that rat?" She said, "Yes, I saw it, but it wasn't a rat. It was a mouse." Mr. Brown said, "I was looking right at it, and it was a rat." Mrs. Brown said, "Henry, I was looking right at it too, and it was a mouse." Mr. Brown said, "I've seen too many rats not to know a rat from a mouse, and it was a rat." Mrs. Brown said, "I've seen just as many rats and mice as you ever did, and it was a mouse, and it ran over behind the wood box." Mr. Brown said, "You are a d--- liar. It was not a mouse."

Mrs. Brown was utterly horrified. In their thirty-eight years of married life, Mr. Brown had never sworn at her, so she angrily packed a suitcase and called a son who lived down the road about six miles to come and get her immediately. She lived with him, and Mr. Brown closed up all of the house except the living room, kitchen and his bedroom. This went on for several weeks, and the neighborhood was much distressed as the Browns were well liked. The neighbors were trying to think of ways to get them back together, and, of course, they were both wishing for reconciliation, but each was too proud to make the first move. A revival started at the church, and the son brought his mother. Mr. Brown attended too. During the course of the revival, and the general good feeling and atmosphere of the revival, plus a little help from the preacher and everyone, a reconciliation was accomplished.

Their first day back home together was a busy one. They opened up all of the windows, aired out the house, scrubbed the floors, and made the house presentable again. That night they sat down before the fire and watched the firelight glow, each pretty much engrossed with his and her own thoughts. Finally Mr. Brown looked over at Mrs. Brown and said, "Mary, what are you thinking about?" Mrs. Brown said, "Henry, I can't help but think how we lived so happily for thirty-eight years. We raised a nice family. We had plenty to live on, and then after all that time we got mad at each other. We separated. We had all the neighbors talking, and all over a little old mouse. Mr. Brown said, "You are a d--- liar. It was a rat." They separated permanently that night, with the question still unsettled: did they separate over a rat or over a mouse?

The Letter Writer

I knew a man of the hills who quite frequently became disgusted with some of the ridiculous things that happen in life, and he would sit down and write a letter to the party or parties concerned. Some of these letters were quite amusing. One of his pet peeves was loan companies and their intense advertising campaigns to loan money, making it seem just as simple as breathing to get a loan. A loan company in Cincinnati made many ridiculous statements, and the following is the letter he sent them.

The Friendly Loan Company
Cincinnati, Ohio

Gentlemen:

I am very gratified with your radio message inviting all who need money to avail themselves of your generous offer to loan money quickly, with no red tape, and in secrecy, without the employer or friends knowing.

This is a very noble gesture on your part, and I am sure that your intentions are of the highest, but in my particular case I would like for you to publicize the loan so that my friends will know that you are taking over as my financial angel. They already know that I will borrow on the slightest opportunity, and it has got to the point where they usually cross the street when they see me coming. If they knew that I had such a wonderful source of supply, as your great financial institution, The Friendly Loan Co., it might be that I could get in speaking distance of them.

As to notifying my employer, don't be silly. If I had an employer I would not be needing a loan, and surely you would not loan money to an employed person, for if they have a job and cannot make ends meet, they certainly would be a poor financial risk. If one is working and cannot break even, he certainly does not know how to budget. If the man who passes on your loans has been passing out money to people who are working, I would suggest that you replace him immediately.

You state in your broadcast advertising that you will loan money to repay the bills, to purchase property, for repairs, or for any worthy cause. My cause is an exceptionally worthy one. I wish to repair the ravages of time and wear to my wardrobe. I am down to my last five suits, and I do feel that since I am out of work that it is necessary to keep up one's morale. I also being out of work have so much time to wear and enjoy good clothing. An employed person has but little time or need for an extensive wardrobe. I know that you will immediately see the need for this loan and that it is an unusually worthy cause, and that it will give you joy to make a loan for so useful a project.

I was particularly impressed by that portion of your advertisement that stated that the borrower could choose a method of repayment to suit his convenience. I would like to repay this at one dollar per year. First, because this would suit my convenience, and second because I always wanted to be a dollar a year man. Washington is full of them, but my politics precludes me getting such an appointment, but at least I could be one in spite of that, with your fine cooperation.

Now it is barely possible that the thought just might enter your mind as to how I could raise the money to repay your loan. It is very simple. I will just call on you for a second loan to repay the first one. You specifically state that you will loan money to repay bills or debts, so it should be a real pleasure for you to do this, and don't forget that delightful thing not mentioned in your broadcast: that little tidbit of 42% interest that you will be making on every transaction. I assure you that I would not be so ungrateful as to go elsewhere to get money when you have been so kind as to make me the original loan. In fact, if the service is as good as you say, I will try to give you all of my business.

We might just start a cycle that would go on and on. In fact by just increasing the amount you will loan to larger sums, and by me giving you all of my business, you could make a career out of me. Just think of the economy involved. Instead of having to pay for all the expensive radio time which you are now doing, and various other forms of advertising, you would be assured of one customer who you could depend on to take all of this money off your hands.

Think of the time and expense it would save you in investigating the people requesting loans. Place pardon the slip. I had forgotten that you state that loans are made without investigation, but think of the time it would save in filing and office work and if you give the prompt and friendly service that you claim, I would be favorably inclined to give you all my business. In fact, I can assure you that you can immediately discontinue advertising for clients.

I do not wish to threaten you, but in case I do not receive my first loan by return mail I will apply to the government for a loan. There is a technicality. I will be compelled to move to a foreign country, as it seems that our government prefers to send our resources aboard, but since that is the case, in the event I do not receive this immediately I will go across the sea, and naturally I will have to add several ciphers to my application for a loan as they do not like to deal in anything but millions or preferably billions, but when they find that I am a foreigner and unemployed they will jump at the opportunity to serve me, and they naturally do not expect or wish it repaid. They only want the worker who pays taxes to pay up promptly so they can continue to be a rich uncle to the world.

I assure you that since I have given you my word earlier in this letter that if you send me a check by return mail that I will give you my business rather than the government. It has always been my motto to give my business to Americans first when possible. I will look forward expectantly to receiving your check by return mail, and the beginning of a long, long haul, we say friendly business relationship.

Yours very truly
Richard Roe
Box 88
Mountain City, W. Va.

Vital Statistics

Just after the turn of the present century one of our hillbillies, who was a stalwart of the political party newly in power, was appointed as head of the Bureau of Vital Statistics. A book could be written on what he did not know about vital statistics, and one sentence could contain his knowledge of this subject, but he was a deserving member of the reigning party, and "to the victor belongs the spoils," so, consequently, he was eligible, and here he was in a nice office with a secretary. He was at a loss what to do with a secretary as he had never dictated a letter in his life, and he had not learned to perch them on his knee. Luckily, a few of the members of his force did, for posterity, record a few facts for the record, but our Bureau Chief chewed his tobacco, and, with a big brass spittoon as his target, drew his salary and thought that the entire set-up was a piece of durn foolishness, except the salary.

One day he received a letter from one of our leading midwestern universities, which went something like this: (It was addressed to the Chief of the Bureau of Vital Statistics, State Capitol Bldg., Charleston, W. Va.)

Dear Sir:

Under a grant of aid from one of the leading philanthropists of this nation we are making a survey of the vital statistics of the United States, and particularly the birth and death rate of the eastern Allegheny and Blue Ridge mountain area, as it is our understanding that, due to the lack of doctors and medical attention, many of the children are being delivered by mid-wives, and we are particularly concerned with the birth and death rate of this particular area, and any statistics which you will be kind enough to give us will be highly appreciated.

Yours very truly
MIDWESTERN UNIVERSITY

Our hero was equal to the occasion. Without the aid of

a secretary, he hand wrote, as we say in the hills, this reply:

Gentlemen:

    I see in your letter where you are trying to find out the vital statistics of the nation, and you seem overly concerned by W. Va. and the mountain section, and you seem to be bothered by the fact that I was delivered by a midwife, and am 57 years old, and could whip a bear with a switch if necessary. A midwife knows more about bringing babies into the world than a carload of these young pipe smoking medical fools with their half baked ideas. If you folks would only forget your book learnin and use the sense that God gives to even the fool geese, you would know that every person that is born has to die whether he lives on the prairies or in the mountains, and whether he is delivered by a fool doctor or a midwife, and so the statistics are exactly the same. For every birth a death, no matter where the Hell it is. Don't bother me with fool questions. If there is any common sense requests you have in the future we will be glad to answer you more fully.

Yours very truly,
Director of Bureau of Vital Statistics

West Virginia Horse Traders

I presume that horse traders all over America had a lot in common and were a breed entirely different from ordinary mortals. I like to think that our own West Virginia horse traders had that little something extra that makes the difference in athletes, evangelists, or any other competitive occupation.

Horse trading is a lost art that went the way of the horse and buggy, and at about the same time, since the people were dependent on a great degree on the horse and buggy.

Our native horse traders were a combination of psychologist, marriage counselor, family doctor, minister and Dale Carnegie, plus the intelligence of the fox and the killer instinct of a wounded tiger. He never traded with you. He planted and nourished the desire in you to trade with him, and he could leave you with a Shetland pony, feeling that in reality it was a sturdy Belgian draft horse suitable for heavy work, and that you had skinned him out of his ears. In many cases he could come back a few months later and do it again, unless you had an iron will.

These men lived a roaming life and neither spun nor toiled, but they lived well, according to mountain standards. Because of their travels, they were always welcome visitors in any mountain home, as they could always give the news of neighboring communities. Lucky was the man who had no horse or pony better than the one ridden or led by the trader; otherwise, in addition to having given him his meals and lodging, he would probably leave with the favorite saddle horse, leaving in its place a wind broken horse or at least an inferior animal.

It is well that these men confined themselves to the fun of horse trading, or they probably would have ended up owning the country.

One old fellow up in the hills told me his experience with a horse trader. He was a mill worker and lived in a rented house. One pay day while he was still in town he encountered a horse trader. He said he didn't know how they got on the subject of horses, but he ended up with a poor excuse of an animal, which in many ways resembled a horse, although he soon found that it had none of the good qualities usually associated with the horse. Also, he discovered that while he was under the charm of this horse trader he had exchanged his pay envlope for this creature, and now he was faced with the ordeal of facing his wife minus his pay check, and with a creature that they needed no more than they needed the black plague. With fear and trembling he went home, leading that wind-broken critter. His wife, with a tongue sharper than a serpent's tooth, gave him a dressing down to end harangues of this nature. She ordered him to return to town immediately and in some way or manner to get this thing off his hands. They had no stable, no feed and no need for such a creature, even if it had been a good specimen of its kind, rather than the scarecrow it was. He said he went back to town and, luckily, found the horse trader and told him his sad story. He said the man listened sympathetically to his tale of woe, and then he said he would be glad to help him. He said he did not know what was said after that, but he ended up with another old plug, and he had taken an order to the saw mill people for his next pay day. However, the horse trade left him with the feeling that he had solved his problem. He went home happy with two misfits instead of one.

He ended his story by saying, "So far as is known, this was the first divorce ever in the history of our family, but that horse trader sure seemed to be a nice feller."

Pay Day In Pax

Prior to the advent of TV and the many forms of entertainment, leisure hours would become quite boring. However, people at least partially solved the problem by playing games, ranging from checkers to baseball. They also enjoyed playing tricks on each other. With the coming of the timber industry, the logging camps were crowded with loggers, and a more hilarious type of entertainment was initiated. After work in the evening, on Sundays and rainy days, the men were crowded together in the log camps without anything to do, so they created their own entertainment. One of the more common types of entertainment was for a couple of participants to verablly abuse the other. It was literally a verbal barrage with each man attempting to outwit or annihilate the other. This was usually done for fun and to the delight of the by-standers.

A few of the participants practiced this until it became an art, for they became adept in vanquishing their opponent. If a stranger happened to be visiting the camp, the participants really put on a show, to the delight of everyone. The winner was the person who could outdo the other in this verbal exchange, with the wittiest, quickest or most devastating come back.

As the camps were closed down, and the men moved on to other camps, the reputations of the more gifted preceded them. Perhaps no one gained a reputation as wide spread as one known as Logger Davis from Nicholas County. No one could recall any occasion that Logger Davis did not have an instant come back. He entered the first World War and immediately gained the same reputation. One of his buddies illustrated his quick wit and thinking with the following story.

Logger Davis did not like to obey camp rules and regulations, and when he was out of sight of officers he would unbutton his shirt, roll his sleeves up, stick his hands in his pockets and otherwise violate regulations.

The buddy stated that he and another soldier were standing in front of the barracks one day when a colonel came along. They saluted as the colonel turned down a side path away from the barracks. The two men happened to look down the path, and they saw Logger Davis coming up the path, shirt unbuttoned, sleeves rolled up, hands in pockets and head down as protection against the wind that was blowing. One said to the other, "He is going to bump into the colonel without seeing him. Let's see what happens." Sure enough, he did not see the colonel until it was too late. The two men were not in hearing distance, but it was evident that the colonel really chewed Logger out, for they could see him straightening up, rolling down his sleeves and buttoning his shirt.

In a few minutes the ordeal was over, and Logger started up the path. One of the men said to the other, "Let's really razz him for getting caught and getting chewed out by the colonel, for there is no way he can get out of this." Logger proceeded up the path, and when he was some fifty feet away he looked up and saw the two with the big smirks on their faces and immediately anticipated what he might be in for. Logger was too quick for them. In a very serious tone, he said, "Boys, I think it's going to be a very short war. I was discussing it with the colonel down there, and he is of the same opinion."

In the early part of the century the most sensational stories of crime and lawlessness that were spread abroad had to do with towns adjacent to the New River gorge, up river from Fayette Station in Fayette County.

Our home was in Greenbrier County, some sixty miles away. We lived in a very tranquil community, for there was no drunkenness or disorder, and even fist fights were few and far between. The stories that came to us from town along the New River gorge were quite something else. The population of that area was made up of many different nationalities and persons of quite different backgrounds. As a result, there was constant friction. Drunkenness, rowdyness, fist fights, gun fights, and robberies were the order of the day. The present TV programs portraying the early days of the wild and wooly west are mild in comparison to the stories of the events that took place in such towns as Thurmond and Pax.

Many people who left these communities tried to tell of the violence that took place, but they soon realized there were not enough descriptive words to do the job and would end up saying it was worse than anything a person could imagine. When words fail, sometimes a comparison can be made with some other disastrous event to illustrate how bad things can be.

A man by the name of Ernest Taylor told a story that made a comparison with the violence in Pax. Mr. Taylor said he was in World War I with a large, good humored man from Pax. That man was not afraid of anything. When the men climbed out of the trenches to face rifle fire, the man from Pax was always among the first and would always be shouting, "Come on, boy, do you want to live forever?"

Near the end of the war the Germans were surrounded and attempted to break through where Taylor and the man from Pax were in the trenches with their outfit. According to Taylor, just as daybreak one morning, the Germans concentrated all their fire power right over their trenches. This included cannon, machine guns, mortars, rifles and other weaponry. This barrage was probably the greatest concentration of fire power ever seen, according to Taylor. In the trenches some of the man were digging deeper, some were hugging the walls, some were praying. However, there was one exception. The man from Pax took out his knife, found a piece of wood, found a comfortable seat and sat unconcernedly whittling. He seemed to be as calm as if sitting in the most tranquil situation.

An officer came crawling slowly up along the trenches and came abreast the man from Pax. The officer paused and said, "Don't you know the battle is getting hotter than Hell up there?" The man from Pax slowly laid down his knife, looked the officer straight in the eye for a moment and then said, "Captain, you haven't seen anything. I would like to have you with me in Pax, West Virginia, some night after pay day."

Lawrence Deitz

BETTY (NUTTER) DEITZ

In Mountain Memories II *I wrote about my mother, Betty (Nutter) Deitz. The following chapters are stories and poems she wrote when she was nearly 100 years old, although a few are from her earlier years.*

The introductory chapter was written by one of her former students, Garnet James Bragg.

Also included is a letter or biography she wrote to me.

Memories

By Garnet James Bragg
Autumn

I like spring, but it's too young.
I like summer, but it's too proud.
So I like best of all autumn, because its leaves are a little yellow, its
   tone mellower, its color richer, and it is tinged with a little
   sorrow.
Its golden richness speaks not of the innocence of spring,
Nor of the power of summer,
But of the mellowness of kindly wisdom of approaching age. It
   knows the limitations of life and its content.

As autumn draws near each year, I can't help but think of the happy days of going to the little country school. We lived quite some distance from school, but we always went the "near way," winding around the hills through the beautiful woods. I used to gather the prettiest leaves I could find and try to keep them by pressing them among the pages of the Sears Roebuck catalogs. But, alas, the leaves always ended up turning brown and breaking to pieces.

How I loved to walk through the woods and enjoy the different scents of drying leaves and the aroma of wildflowers! I can't help but feel sorry for the children who missed living in the country — having the joy of walking in the paths of golden sunlight that illuminated the radiant colors of maples, oaks, poplars and many other trees, or taking the time to swing on a grapevine once in a while. The days seemed endless, and no one was in a hurry.

Autumn was the time of year that reminded us that school was just around the corner. When we thought of school time, it meant clothes and a lunch bucket (our lunch bucket was a lard pail — there were no cafeterias or hot lunches; we took our own). Children were not clothes conscious, as they are today; clothes were a necessity to us, rather than a way to keep in style and wear "brand names." My mother made most of our clothes, and she always managed to have a new dress for me in time for the first day of school. Thank goodness, we weren't judged by our clothes! I really don't think we paid much attention to each other's attire. Our main interest was to get together and share all we had done throughout the summer.

Our school was only one room, and I have many times wondered if teachers of today could cope with teaching children in all grades, from primer through eighth grade, all in one room. How did the teacher in my day take little ones who were starting in their first year and teach the ABC's, while going on through all the other grades and ages? These teachers had to comfort the little ones, letting them know that they could indeed go home at the end of a school day, and that they weren't being held prisoner. I'm sure the teachers had to wipe many a tear and lots of noses as they tried to explain what school was all about.

The in-between grades seemed to take so much time and patience, with the teacher trying to keep everyone interested. But the teacher I remember who was exceptional and wise, our friend first and then our teacher, was Mrs. Betty Deitz. Many times she took little children on her lap to console them with a story. Soon they would become so absorbed in listening to her that I'm sure the children soon forgot they were in school.

Most of the students had quite a distance to walk to school, so winter time found us bundled up to keep warm. When we started for home after school, Mrs. Deitz saw to it that we had our clothes fastened, hoods on our heads, and galoshes on the right feet.

Our school days were happy times, and Mrs. Deitz made them so. She was a firm teacher, and we soon understood that we were there to learn. When we were learning our multiplication tables, Mrs. Deitz said the student who learned the tables first would get a prize. I went to bed at night repeating those tables, and started again the first thing in the morning. My mother got so tired of hearing them over and over that she said she would give me a prize if I could learn to say them to myself!

Well, I won the multiplication table prize that year, and Mrs. Deitz gave me a beautiful little book with a bright yellow cover, titled *Little Sir Galahad*. I kept this treasure for many years and spent many hours exploring the delights between its covers.

Mrs. Deitz had many ways to keep us interested. Even we who were in the higher grades would listen when she was teaching the younger ones. I'm sure the Lord set her aside to be a teacher when she was born.

We girls used to build playhouses out of rocks and moss that grew close by the schoolhouse, which was built on the edge of a beautiful woods. We usually used our noon hour to play in our pretend houses with bits of broken dishes or other castoff items brought from home. We didn't have to worry about carpeting for our houses, for nature provided every color imaginable, from the brilliant reds and oranges to the subtleness of gold and brown leaves. More than likely our houses didn't last the day for several of the boys could always be counted on to sneak around and wreck the product of all our hard labors. Mrs. Deitz could be counted on to administer a good scolding.

We all loved and respected Mrs. Deitz, and her word was law to us. Our parents instilled in us that we were to give her our respect and to obey her; if not, trouble would be waiting at home.

I had the privilege of having both Mr. and Mrs. Deitz as teachers, but I spent more years with Mrs. Deitz than any other teacher.

I loved to spend time at the Deitz home, and I went there as often as I could. I remember the many books they had, and I always felt free to borrow any I wished to read. I was never satisfied with just one book, for I was an avid reader, so I usually headed home with several books under my arm. My mother would be disgusted because she couldn't get me to do anything as long as I had an unfinished book around.

The Deitz home was a rambling two-story house with plenty of room to play. "Blind Man's Bluff" and hide and seek were favorites. We would head upstairs after the chores were done and proceed to almost tear the house down. Mr. and Mrs. Deitz never seemed to hear us.

One time when we were playing hide and seek we nearly tore the house apart trying to find my brother who had been hidden by one of the girls. My brother had been placed across the head of the bed with a feather bolster over him (a bolster was a long pillow that took the place of two pillows). We finally had to abandon our search and, needless to say, my brother and his "hider" were elated.

I can't ever remember hearing Mrs. Deitz complain or say anything harmful about another person. I knew her for many years, and even after she was in her twilight age with failing health, she always had a twinkle in her eyes and a wonderful sense of humor. I visited her after she had been in the hospital and had the privilege of reading some of her poetry. She had quite a stack of different pieces she had written. Mrs. Deitz was nearing her 100th birthday at this time, but her mind was as keen and sharp as ever. We talked of the days when she had taught school, and she still remembered most of the children's names who had attended her classes.

I still have the letter Mrs. Deitz wrote me when my husband passed away. She had decided to write me a letter instead of sending the usual sympathy card. Her words gave me such comfort.

She urged me to have courage and to take solace in my children, that God would take care of everything. She said a way would be made for folks who tried. I realized Mrs. Deitz knew how it was to be left alone with children to finish raising them. Even though it's been twenty-one years, I still have this wonderful letter. Mrs. Deitz was a wise, compassionate person.

In looking back at my life, I wish I had told Mrs. Deitz how much she meant to me. I think she knew though, that I always held her in the highest esteem. Too often it seems we hesitate to let others know how much they mean to us.

I will always remember Mr. and Mrs. Deitz with much affection and respect. They were both wonderful people who made my life better for knowing them. They are a big part of my childhood memories.

By Betty Nutter Deitz

To you young folks seventy years seem like a long time but really it's not long at all. In fact it seems only like yesterday when I was a small girl, just as you are all today. If you will listen and sit right still I'll tell you about some of the yesterdays that took place right here on this self same farm, but not in the same house.

Right out beyond the far corner of the garden there, where the grass is greenest, is where father and mother lived when they first went to housekeeping. An old log house stood on that tiny knoll, of which I will tell you later along. The old stone chimney was at the upper side of the house, and in the little hollow by the big oak was a deep spring. A huge barrel served to hold the cool bubbling water.

We children liked to play under the green oak, where we made an old timey play house of rocks, filling the sides with green moss which we carried from the forest. We gathered the acorn caps and used them for kitchen utensils. I think we enjoyed making mud pies and poking around for crayfish in the deep holes just as small boys and girls do today.

We lacked many of the conveniences in our yesterdays that we enjoy today and everybody was kept very busy trying to help make a living. We had no factories to weave our cloth, not many new shiny shoes, and most of the good things we now have to eat were unheard of. We made our sugar from maple trees of the forests. Our fruits were dried because we had no jars, and we had never heard of breakfast cereal. But by the time I was ten years of age a few of these things were to be found on the market.

Our mothers had home-made looms in almost every home and a small as well as a large spinning wheel. All of our floor coverings were made from old rags torn into long strings and woven into strips of carpet on the big loom in the corner.

Maybe you would like to know what we wore instead of pretty colored anklets and the silk hose like you girls have to wear.

I'll tell you about our old mare named Dolly. Now old Dolly came in awfully handy. In fact she served as an all purpose horse on our farm, but she must have been imposed upon for she had a vicious temper for some reason. I can just dimly remember when I was sent to the spring for water and suddenly old Dolly pounced at me with her fore-feet in the air, her ears flat against her head and her white teeth shining. The balance of my memories of the accident is only from say so's, but I do remember my long rest in the big tall bed, and the neighbors dropping in to see me, and especially my small tin cup of coins given to cheer me up, I suppose. Money was scarce in my yesterdays, compared to your todays.

Maybe you would like to hear about the old folks of the yesterdays. When thinking about them now, it seems to me like every one was old then. Even our Daddys wore long beards. I often think of the aged women both far and near and know how they liked to visit with one another.

Every family had at least a few sheep, but instead of sending the wool off to market as is done now, Mother had it washed in soap-suds, but a lot of hard work came before that could be done. First, green wood from the forest had to be chopped and burned. Then the ashes from the wood was placed in what we called an ash-hopper, which was something like a huge barrel with no bottom, placed on a table-like stone. Then we all carried water, pouring it into the hopper a little at a time, while it slowly dripped into a container below the stone. This water we called lye, but it still was far from being soap. As I said, we all had to work hard back then and save also. You see we could not afford to buy lard or grease of any kind with which to make our soap.

When the hogs were killed in the fall of the year our Mother saved everything excepting the squeal. While the men gathered to do the butchering the women took care of the waste material, even cleaning and washing the entrails. Sometimes in the process of the long cold day away from the warmth of the fire, they froze their fingers and toes. No wonder it took more than one petticoat at such times, as well as red flannels to keep out the cold.

Now going back to the lye and the wool washing. All this waste from butchering was thrown into large iron kettles hung over a great outdoor fire. The lye was added. The kettles were filled with water and there it boiled away until the mixture turned out to be a soft soap, which cut the dirt from chapped hands to a frizzle. Then more and more hard work came before the sheep's wool could be made clean, washed through many tubs of soapy water and was ready for more hand labor in getting it ready for children's clothing. I wonder now how our parents dressed us at all. I am sure our mothers must have been very patient, don't you? For she is only getting a good start toward the dozen small pairs of stockings she has to have ready for us to wear through the deep snow to school. You see, after the wool is washed and dried, then it has to be taken in small handfuls and combed into long round strings about the size and shape of that chair round. Mothers then moved to the spinning wheel and drew that wool out into long threads. Back and forth, back and forth she walked, sometimes all day and far into the night. As the wool is slowly spun into yarn it is also wound on to a spindle. It seems to you, I am sure, that nothing more can be done, but the yarn must be colored, and perhaps there is no dye to be had. In that case, Mother must take bark from a walnut tree and make a brown like dye. Then she must color the yarn and knit the hose. I am afraid you girls of today would refuse to wear them after all. They are as thick and heavy as the leather in our pocketbooks of today and not at all pretty. You can see that providing clothing during the yesterdays was a long and tiresome process. But boys and girls of your age were required to learn the process as book education did not then seem so important.

Suppose we take a look at that steep hill field below the big road. Most of the fields that you can see above look to me much as they do today but that one steep field holds many childhood memories for me yet. I must have been about four years old when father began felling the big trees and clearing the land on this side of the field next to the house. It is only a dim dream to me. When the work first started, you can see that it must have been another one of those endless jobs. Yet, in the process I was five, six, yes seven or eight years old. Almost the first thing I can recall about the hillside was of my baby brother and me carrying our small pails of water to father as he crossed back and forth with the big plow drawn by a yoke of oxen. Many of the long rounds around the field made with one or the other of us sitting up between the handles of the big plow. We thought it was a grand ride, and Father always enjoyed whatever we children loved. Coming in from the field in small groups all covered with grime and their clothes dripping with perspiration, yet a jolly and hungry bunch, as they file in a long line to the big trough of water below the spring, carrying their soap and towels. From there this long line fell in place at the big table, which is loaded down with more things to eat than we ever see today. Mother had added some kind of contrivance to our every day table in order to lengthen it into a board to accommodate so many hungry men. After the dinner was finished, Mother and the neighbor women took over the big dish washing job. The table was again put in order while women and children fill in the places left vacant by the men. Men are so exhausted by their long and heavy morning work. But it wasn't quite so funny when all was ready for the slow job of gathering the brush and sticks and piling them into great heaps ready to be burned. This was more work than play, even for us children at this particular time. But neither joy nor sorrow lasts forever, and we had a lot of fun when the big log rolling day came around.

Maybe you would like for me to tell you about this. I haven't forgotten the log rolling on the far side of the field by any means. By the time Father got that far I must been seven years old.

Anyway the big day came, the first of its kind that I can recall, for you must remember that I was a mere child. Great preparations were made to feed every one. I wonder now what we would do if we had to make preparations to feed twenty or twenty-five hungry men with all thoughts of a store or store bought food out of the question. Anyway it had to be done during our yesterdays. Big buckets of corn pone, as we call it, were made by an old recipe and set to sweeten in a warm place. I don't know now what we called it when ready for the oven. We might have said "hatched" but I really have forgotten. Anyway, mother had a huge baker of heavy iron with lid to match. The red hot wood ashes were then pulled onto the stone hearth. The oven with the corn pone sit on the hot ashes and covered all over with more and more ashes. These were changed from time to time until the pones were brown and crisp, and really delicious in taste. I am sure if we had to go through all these ashes and dirt to produce a pone of bread now, that we would say "It makes me nervous," or "I'm nervous enough to scream." But if Mother had stopped to scream at this time, I'm afraid a lot of work would have gone undone, for there were great loaves to bake and dozens of dried apple pies to be made, all in the slow way. Then there was the big fat sheep that Father had butchered to be cooked and stored away in the stone jar down in the cool spring house, while we children must be sent to our grandmothers to borrow dishes, knives and forks, and to our nearest neighbors to invite the old ladies who would have felt really hurt if left out of the picture.

We are all up bright and early on log rolling mornings. I see Grandfather now as he appeared at the break of day on his big gray horse, but soon more and more men came, most of them on horseback. By seven or eight o'clock they had all arrived. Some of our nearest neighbor women came early also to help Mother with the dinner, some of our cousins to help us children to carry water to the men. We were kept very busy. I don't think horses ever drank so much water as the men did that day. The big logs were sawed and rolled into great heaps until the entire landscape took on a different look with each trip we children made with the buckets of water. It was very interesting to me to watch the men at their work. How they sweated and lifted and heaved, but I am sure they had some fun amid it all, for they took time to tell jokes, and their peals of laughter echoed through space. One big fellow that must have thought he was the giant of the crowd often took time to just stop and send out a great yell that almost shook the trees and gave us children many thrills. But I think everyone enjoyed the dinner hour most of all. It makes me sad just now as I review that noon hour scene. I can plainly see the men as they fall fast asleep beneath the shade of the big oak that you can see across there at the end of the garden. Now I am sure I have told you enough about long rolling day.

But more than anything else we children enjoyed the night a few months later when several of the neighbors came back and helped father burn the great heaps of logs. We children sat on the big stone that you can see out there in the orchard till far after midnight, watching the streams of red sparks as they sparkled and snapped in the air.

When I see the same trees standing in place after all these years, the self same stone in the old orchard, the same land marks over the old farm, it makes me really lonely. I am not brave enough to search in my mind for a single one of the men or women that came to help us with our tasks back in the faraway yesterdays.

I am sure that as you boys and girls look upon life it seems very far away, but on looking back, it's much like a dream. Some of it bad, some good, but we won't dwell on that part.

We were talking about that old hillside field. Just look at it now, grown up, full of briers and scrub brush, after all the hard work. Oh! Yes, it did have one blessing, and that is the deep sulphur spring right down below the scrub brush along the tall trees.

After Father got the trees cut, the logs burned, the brush all picked up, the rocks piled in big heaps, the rough ground plowed, he decided to plant it in corn. No sooner was the corn planted than the little chipmunks or ground squirrels came, from every crevice and hole it seemed to devour the newly planted corn. Father spent hours each night it seems in making what he called triggers for traps to set for the pests. My brother and I got quite expert in setting the traps, but the more squirrels we killed the more came. Then father decided to send us children with pans and sticks much like drums. We were in the field at break of day making as much noise with our equipment as an entire army. I am not sure whether we succeeded in frightening the small pests to death, but I am sure we must have learned a valuable lesson in patience as we continued the rounds up hill and down for days. Our feet grew sore, and in the early morning hours our fingers were half frozen. Maybe this seemed almost too much for small children, but not to be compared with the long hours and months during which father had labored to get ready the big field. Father always compensated us children by helping us to get some fun along with our work. We pulled up the weeds and thinned the corn. We often found the cool water and the shade of the big trees pleasant. I remember how much fun we would get out of pushing one another's heads deep in the water as we were stooping over drinking from the spring. If this game did not raise our spirits or make us forget we were tired we would often take half an hour in the shade for a game of hide and seek, father being the most active and interested party of the game.

After the big field was planted down in grass and turned over to the farm stock, life went along much easier on the farm for all of us. In fact, the other fields were easily kept under control, and when not supervised, my small brother and I found much pleasure time on our hands.

We were very fond during the summer months of hunting over the farm for the big hornets' nests. We made torches on the ends of long poles and had the fun of burning these. Father was always on the lookout for a joke to play on us children. He awoke one morning very early, and there stood the tall stump near the gate burning away. It had caught fire on the previous day along with the big nest of hornets clinging to its side. Father got us out of bed in a hurry that time by making us think the big haystack had been consumed by the blaze along with the hornets' nest and stump. However, his object was to hurry us kids off over the hilltop for the cows, but driving the cows home did not always prove comfortable, and yet it is a childish memory I still cherish. On one such trip over the hill and through the woods I learned most of my lessons in nature. I sometimes shed my tears along in sympathy with the mother robin that had been robbed of her babies by the snakes that were real pests in that day. Brother and I managed to see all the small grass people. On many cold mornings when the dew lay heavy on the grass, we found the spider webs woven into the most beautiful nets, and so delicate in texture that we tried to avoid spoiling them with our footsteps, but we did not then know that small insects wove these nets or webs from a secretion or saliva of their own bodies. We did not always linger to see all such things for often our bare feet ached with cold and our small toes were as red as rosebuds.

One day as we were strolling right on top of that high knob we saw over at the right at least a dozen of our cattle. All at once it seemed to have popped into my small brother's mind to take a ride and on to the neck of a big steer he jumped as quick as a wink, but just as quickly the whole drove of cattle stampeded down the slope and around the side of the knob.

I should have been frightened, but I took it as the order of the day, racing across the knob to see the outcome. The cows were issuing bellows as they ran, with the colt following in the rear. By the time the entire procession reached the small flat by the walnut tree, off slid brother as whole and happy as ever.

When father had to be away from home, much of the time brother and I tried mixing work and pleasure, perhaps four fifths pleasure and one fifth work. It was real fun walking the old zig zag rail fence. The game was to start at one corner of the field and see which one could make the entire round, getting the fewest falls. We got enough practice out of this that we should have been expert rope walkers.

Then I have to laugh when I think of the big field back of the hill, maybe 20 acres in all. We called it our promised land field, but it didn't look very promising that summer that father had planted it all in corn and then got himself a more profitable job than farming. The Big Promised Land field left all to itself proceeded at once to produce, but not corn, just sprouts and brush and big weeds in abundance. On and on they grew, ankle high, knee high, shoulder high. At last father came home one weekend and took us two kids over to the Promised Land field with hoes. He offered us fifty cents apiece if we would clean it all up. How we did want to earn all that money. All in good faith we started along cutting diligently for a least ten minutes before we wanted a drink of water from the cold spring over the hill. By that time the sun was hot, and of course it would be much pleasanter in the shade. So we chose a spot for work under the chance tree left standing in the field. From that we decided the upper side of the field would be so much nicer, so we changed positions again and this time cut through at least ten feet more from end to end of our rows. We began to think we were very hungry and decided to go see if we could find some golden sweet apples in the old deserted orchard a half mile away. But we just couldn't make up our minds to let all the money pass, so we played and worked at intervals until father came home. When he reviewed our work he said the Promised Land field looked to him very much like a checker board with many large, and a few very small dots scattered here and there. How he did laugh, but at that we probably had accomplished more than he expected of us. We had learned quite a lot about birds, toads, lizards and snakes. More than that, we had learned to climb trees like a couple of monkeys.

From this time, father's job kept him away from home a great deal, and as we children grew older and able to help with the farm work, mother took over, making us a very good overseer. But our Promised Land field soon went the way of the old hill side and was turned to the farm animals for grazing around.

You say you want to hear more about our clothing. You see, new styles are adopted with every new generation, perhaps more often. When I was about eight years old and old timey folks wore fully gathered long skirts and slowly changed their appearance. The days of the hoop skirts had come. The hoops started near the waist line, being placed along at intervals nearly to the bottom of the skirt. I can only imagine how the girls then looked, probably like they were wearing huge umbrellas reaching from waist line down.

What I can't imagine though is how they managed to sit down. Maybe you can figure that out. Then came the over-skirt day, which I sorta remember of thinking quite pretty with the dozens of puckers, pleats and gathers in the smaller, shorter skirt worn over another of longer length. But I can clearly recall the days of the bustle style. This was nothing more than a large pad made to fit the form and taste of each individual and worn in the back and near the top of the skirt, sort of over the top of the hips. Sometimes these pads were stuffed with cotton padding, and some of the girls were accused of using sawdust or bran for the stuffing of their bustles. Anyway, that is what a few of the more mischievous young men told. Thinking about it now, these skirts seem to have been quite unnecessary and cumbersome. In fact, I can recall a lot of times of being thrown from a frightened horse and was so tangled in the long black thing, called a riding skirt, that I can't imagine how I escaped with my life. Then again, I remember finding my big skirt so laden with mud that I almost toppled over. But you remember I told you we were so modest that we dare not show our ankles. But the time came in the by and by when the side saddle gradually faded out of the picture and women began riding men's saddles and man's fashion also. But any of your mothers can recall that day we were in the days of yesteryear only one jump ahead of the covered wagon. Most people provided themselves with a horse and two styles of saddles, one for men and another for women. Most of you can often see men's saddles still in use, but I doubt if any of you children have seen an old timey woman's saddle with two horns on the front and large leather skirt on the left side. One of my chief pleasures during at least half of my life was horseback riding. Everybody traveled in the same fashion, the men often with large saddle bags fastened back of them. The women rode sideways, as we called it then. Even we small girls, as well as other women were provided with great skirts in solid black color, gathered very full at the waist line and reaching almost to the ground. These skirts were intended to keep your dresses clean. We slipped them off at the end of our destination and hung them across our saddles.

All the old ladies dressed in the same styles, with long skirts gathered full at the waist line and dragging the ground all around. The waists were made to fit quite snug back then, I suppose to add to their comfort. They wore what we call petticoats made usually from white material and in the same style as the outer skirt. Often more than one petticoat was worn at a time, so you can see our mothers and grandmothers looked rather barrel-like from the waist to the floor. No one ever got even a peek at an ankle. In fact, when I was fifteen years old I still blushed if any one said ankle in my presence and would probably have fainted if he had said knee instead. You see, we were really modest in the yesterdays. I don't mean for you to think that our bodies were left out in the cold, for most of our grandmothers of that day wore red flannels in winter and white flannels in the summer time, made to fit the body snug and provided with sleeves reaching to the wrists. I am not sure whether we were allowed to say the word wrists or not, but I do know how people wore home knit wrist bands of heavy flannel.

Maybe you would like for me to tell you about my great-grandmother. To me, all old ladies looked just about the same as she did, at least they wore the same kind of bonnets, dresses, shoulder shawls, and used some kind of wooden cane or stick for support.

Great-grandmother died when I was about ten years of age, she then having passed her hundredth birthday by a few years. You know everyone grows shorter when she gets very aged and, to me, grandmother was really very short, but I can almost see her now as she plodded along the hot road with her cane, and I remember Mother always sending one of us children to lay the fence down for her, even to the very last rail, then to lead her to the house. She never failed to wear a dress with a barrel-like skirt and a checkered home-woven shawl around her shoulders, as all women wore in that day. Then she wore a large black bonnet, with full gathered ruffles held in place on top with paste board stays. Then beneath all this head wear, she wore a dainty white cap, changing it at bed time to what we called night caps.

During my first year in school I can remember of great-grandmother's visit to our school. She had reached her second childhood long before this, so she marched in quite bravely and was ushered by the teacher to a near by seat. We tried hard to hold back the giggles when she began to recite aloud, "Ding dong bell, Cat in and well." And other Mother Goose rhymes. But best of all, grandmother was a pioneer, and we children often heard tales of how bravely she carried on, even during the days of Indians and wild beasts.

My Little Big Dennis

By Betty Deitz

As I look back to that year of 1913 I wonder how a new baby managed to survive. I think I (your Mom) was your chief stay and support, and you sure were leaning on a broken stick. I had simply worked myself threadbare through the previous summer. I was on the brink of a breakdown physically and mentally, a poor time for a new baby to get his first glimpse of this hard world. No wonder you let out such a yell of protest. Winter was so soon on the way, our new house was nice, and I can say airy, clean and cold, cold, and almost empty.

We moved out of the hen house where they teased you by saying you were the only one born in a hen's nest. Maybe that was why you were tough.

Not too long after we moved into the new house, Granville and Faye came from school with the whooping cough. Six of you, all to bark away time, and a job to keep you all warm. Watson and I took time about sitting up at night, lifting the arms of six of you, to keep you from choking. You proved the toughest of them, and so you got along the best.

The hurry scurry of spring came at last, with gardens to start and fruit to can. All of you went along to the strawberry field. You lay on a blanket, and old Rover lay near you so that no harm came. The others could gather berries, unless it was Helen. She could ramble. Even with an extra member in the family, this summer was not quite so hectic as the last, though the big house seemed to invite company.

That was the fall that Bob Hunt decided with Watson's consent that our living room would be a good place to collect taxes. Tax payers came from all quarters by horseback and buggy. Of course, it was too far to drive without food, so we fed them.

Bob was better than anyone else to pay board. He left $2.00 on Watson's desk at the end of his three days' stay, and he made up for any over by bragging on how cute you were (I agreed). You were good in addition. You and I spent many cold days in the new kitchen. You were wrapped in a blanket on chairs by the side of the stove, as there was no room in by the fire for the visitors. The stove smoked, and we got choked up, but I didn't know it was the sulphur from the coal. In spite of all you grew in strength and knowledge!

Bob came twice each fall for six years, always bragged on how cute you were, and that paid the bill.

Politicians, sheep buyers and passersby didn't pay that much. Everyone was welcome in that day, whenever he dropped in.

Rosa wanted me to give her one of my half dozen. Like the poem, "Which Shall It Be?" Sometimes she would borrow you or Helen or Irene. They didn't like the change, but you seemed to, so we lost you for short periods. We missed you.

I am not sure but through the years you were also the "goodest," Lawrence the best worker, and Granville the smartest, or we thought so, maybe because he was the first.

We were busy enough that your school days came before we knew it. From the first you liked math. I never had a complaint from one of your teachers. You were a good boy, Dennis, always. That meant more than anything to me.

I think you children as a rule enjoyed the farm. I was busy, especially in summer, but I enjoyed your games. It kept you, Irene and Helen busy moving your playhouse from the well house loft, to the granary loft, to the big organ box, and I guess you can remember the big limb of the apple tree that had bent nearly to the ground. You and Helen fought over which would get the limb to play "Whip the Cat."

Soon I found myself moving fast to get all tasks done. I really don't know whether I was coming or going. It was a job to keep you all clothed for school, and church.

I must have thought it a sin if any kind of fruit wasted from Bingham to the Albon Nutter place. Anyway, I left you (then only two years of age) and rode horseback to Jake Nutter's and over a rattlesnake infested hillside and gathered huckleberries all day. When I got back to your granddad's farm, there you sat astride the fence, looking for your careless Mom. I had trusted you with Irene and Helen. You didn't stay put. I still wonder at the risks I took, scrambling over rocks, hills and ridges to feed my flock.

Another event I recall is when you were about four years old, and I sent you to Mother's to borrow something. You met Cardia Haynes on the way, and she stopped to talk to so cute a little boy. She said, "Hello, where did you pop up? Where are you going? What for? Etc. and so on." Then, "What is your name anyway?" Suddenly the quiz grew old, so you answered, "I'm not telling you my name, and I don't care what yours is." (Sorta crude, weren't you?)

If you disappeared, the best place to look would be in the top of an apple tree or on top of a building. You were a little climber from the first.

You weren't infected with a real bad temper. Thank the Lord for that, and you slid along through school. No fusses with your schoolmates or teachers. You went to school to me one year in your early teens. You knew math better than your teacher, so I knew better than to tackle a problem you were stalled upon. When you were ready for high school, I don't know if I could have managed without Faye's help, and especially Rosa's later on. Then I thought you could make it if I could just manage to send you one year to college. You lacked one year in English. Mr. Lanum just gave you credit. But how did you manage on $25.00 a month to pay your tuition, room and board? You and Faye were the ones that counted the scarce penny. I had to count pennies too at that time, but not as carefully as before I went to teaching steady in 1923. My highest salary ever was $85.00; Watson's too.

You tried selling magazines one summer, then to work in a store. You could have taught from having one year in college, but you chose not. From now on Madeline took you over and did a good job. I am proud of you.

Love, Mom

My Dear Little Pearl

The Seventh To Arrive
By Betty Nutter Deitz

The day Pearl came was on December 13, 1915. The snow lay deep on the ground, and the weather man said it was almost zero. Our big farm house was cold and drafty. That Monday morning came in with more than its usual hustle-bustle — four or five children to be gotten off to school, and Watson not knowing what to do about a load of produce he had to deliver for the Meadow River Company. He ran to the phone every five minutes. Mother was with us, and so was a hired girl. The breakfast table was full, and I felt I had to get away from the mob, so I ran upstairs and climbed into a cold, cold bed and went into chills. As a result we had to call the doctor and difficulties arose of every kind. I can't describe further, but I was surprised at last when my little girl arrived alive after agonizing hours.

Dear Little Pearl. She was the quiet one. I can't recall of ever hearing her cry. If I had to leave home I could look for her little face at the window, always watching, never saying a word or making complaints. She knew where everything in the house belonged, or if lost, could be found. "Just ask Pearl," everyone said. She left out her "D's" when talking. Lawrence was Bosh; Dennis was Dash.

The other children seemed to be ready for school at the age of five, so when school started, I sent Pearl. It may have made her nervous. Anyway, when she had only gone to school three days, she came home real sick. We called a doctor, but he knew nothing of what was wrong and gave her medicine for worms. (That's what he gave for everything.) As always, she did not complain — just wanted her Mommy. Always it was, "Mommy, come here." "Get me a good cold drink." I loved to do all this for her, and I never tired, day or night. She was so sweet and patient. In six weeks she was able to sit up and satisfy herself with the Sears Roebuck catalogue. I was behind with everything, so we sat in by the fire, she with the catalogue, and I making my sewing machine hum. I gave her the privilege of selecting a Christmas present for each member of our family, which I ordered. She was so happy and could walk only by holding onto the wall or something. I little dreamed that at Christmas I would be begging God to take her out of her pains.

On the day before Thanksgiving I was worried about the next day's dinner. How little to worry about, I realized when Pearl had a relapse the next morning.

I saw at bedtime that my little girl was having trouble again. I allowed her to sleep with me, but I didn't sleep. By four o'clock in the morning I was so uneasy that I got up and took her in my arms and sat by the fire. At eight o'clock the mail carrier came, and I sat Pearl on a chair near me while I wrote a bill for her medicine. All of a sudden she threw herself into my arms, her eyes seemed to jump out and from that time on, Thanksgiving Day, until January 5, she went from convulsions, one to another (between unconsciousness). Her legs and arms constantly drew up and then stretched until she wore the skin into sores. She never spoke a word and maybe never heard a sound. If she recovered she would be a vegetable. So, here was my prayer with my broken heart.

My prayer was: "Oh, Lord, why did this happen? Please take her, Lord, out of her pain. I don't want her to live a vegetable, never to be her sweet little self. Oh, Lord, please, please take her — it's her birthday. She was so sweet, take her as a present, and I'll try to never forget." So went my prayers, day and night, for six or seven weeks. If she had lasted longer, I would have gone with my dear little girl. Some things are worse than death.

Greed

By Betty Nutter Deitz

As I sit alone and wonder about so many things, I think old Satan must have come to lower the advent of man on this old planet earth. The very earliest history of man shows that he was born with a sense of greed. We have no way of knowing about whether they argued and fought over who should occupy the best and biggest cave, but I'm inclined to think they did, for as man grew in numbers and knowledge, so has he grown in greed. The Bible says the love of money is the root of all evil. At present money means gold, silver or its equivalent. In the past there was mostly an exchange of goods or products for exchange, but the desire was in man to make the best bargain, get the best of his fellow man if possible, otherwise, he was not smart. Envy is one trait of character that has led to the world's distress. Neighbors have quarreled, people murdered, and all wars or about all wars, have been the result of mass greed, mostly for the desire to possess. To possess has led to theft, lying, even killing. It all leads back to greed.

Greed even reached into heaven. Satan envied the throne (according to Bible history) enough so that he organized a rebellion, secured one-third of the angels and was cast onto this old earth. Here he carries on his greed through his influence on man.

Money, money, money, the song of the ages! When gold is discovered any place on this earth, what a rush it causes. Men risk starvation, death and destruction to reach the spot first. Even at this late date, when we should have learned a lesson. We rushed to California where someone had found gold dust. We froze to death in Alaska to be the first to get our fingers into the pie, and so shall it be to the end of time, as long as Satan is ruler in hell. He knows when and where to poke his nose into man's mind and business. He is well aware of the weak spot in every man's character and how to attack that weak spot. Not only does he know where but when. Old Satan is no fool, but we can be grateful that we have a strong line of defense, a kind of providence that comes to our assistance, but without full confidence in that providence, we often are tempted and fail.

The Other Side Of Man

In spite of man's greed and jealousies, he has a deep seated desire for the good of humanity. He is a two-sided creature, a mixture of good and bad. In my time I have seen wars fought, a nation declared by us, *all evil.*

The war ended, and the face of the nation entirely changed for the good. For instance, we might look at Japan. Our highest enemy, not fit for hell. The war ended and Japan was our ally and friend.

So it is in all walks of life. We might call this generosity. America has always been known for its generosity, which is often taken for granted, with no thanks thrown in. "America will come to our rescue," is the hope and song of the world. To me, I fear we have almost given away our birthright. As with individual people, so it is with nations. They learn to take the easiest road out. They lose their independence and drift toward being parasites. Then they more or less blame it on the very ones who helped them pull their chestnuts out of the fire, through their own generosity. Hard knocks have founded more *wisdom* than any university.

The Intelligence Of Animals

By Betty Deitz Nutter

Man is supposed to be the most gifted of all animal kind, but many animals have gifts that man does not in general possess. Some people call it instinct, but, to me, it seems deeper than that.

What makes the ant so wise? Why does it store food for its winter use? Why does he keep a sentry to watch at all times? How does each individual ant know exactly its job? How does the bee know to take the most direct route to its home? How does it know to protect the queen bee and obey her directions, and a thousand other questions about the wisdom of bees?

Every animal is equipped with ways and means of defending itself. A horse either runs or uses its heels. In a fierce storm a horse will turn his heels to the storm. Cattle use their horns for defense, and you will see them facing a storm, turn their heads in that direction. The rabbit and the deer and some other animals will use their swift feet, and thus escape danger by running. How do the bear and the groundhog know to eat much food before winter and thus store up fat so they can hibernate or go into their long winter's sleep? How do ducks and various other birds know the time and place for their migration in order to find food? These are just a few of the questions that make me ask how wise are the ways of the animal kingdom?

Let us look at the eel for a second. They all look alike. Some are found on the coasts of New England, some in the Mediterranean, and some near Norway, but all go to the same spot and in the same season to spawn, or hatch their young. Then when their task is done, they die. How do the young when mature know just where their parent eels came from and make their way through thousands of miles of sea, and without fail find the home of their parents' home waters? (This is more than a mystery to me.)

About as much can be said for the seal. They travel all cold water seas, go to the same place to bear their young, and never get lost. A big bull seal selects himself a territory and herds his wives there and then dares any other bull seal to come near one of his cows, at the risk of his life. So some animals have a sense of jealousy. Even the wild stud horse has killed many of his enemies because of his jealous streak.

I think from observation that maybe all animals have some way of communicating with their kind, and sometimes I wonder if they think and plan. I know of one mother cat which had to have planned ahead. The stork had about a month previously left her one little white kitten. Mother cat had to take particular care of her only baby, so she hid it high in the garret loft, where she could manage to get in by way of a ladder. A bad boy came along and threw the ladder onto the ground. What could mother cat do? It would be just too difficult to carry a mouse, a bird, or anything to her baby, and even harder to jump to the ground. One day later I was by my bedroom window when I saw a white object hit the ground, and another one followed a second later. It was mother cat. She had carried her kitten and thrown it down on its feet. She followed, but what was funny was that she ran, carrying her kitten by the back of the neck, ran like lightning, and pitched her kitten down a post hole. I knew she had the place looked over and planned ahead. Her movements were too swift and sure.

Do animals think and plan?

Small Narrations Of Dogs And Their Intelligence

By Betty Nutter Deitz

A neighbor had a dog that somehow sensed that I was afraid and came to comfort me, or to try to still my fears. I was afraid of ghosts and thought they inhabited every corner and every dark room. We were a newly-married couple and moved to a small village where everyone had his particular ghost story to tell. I often went for a short visit to a neighbor's house where there was a large, heavily-wooled yellow dog. Sometimes I would relate my fears of ghosts when my husband would be gone after dark or perhaps all night. The dog, "Old Wolfe," must have understood, for he suddenly went home with me and followed me from place to place. At night he slept under the house and managed to get as nearly beneath my bed as possible. He would often tap his tail to let me know he was there, but this did not lessen my fear of ghosts as long as we lived in this palce. This dog stayed with me until his folks moved, and they wanted good "Old Wolfe." How did he read my fears?

The second dog that I particularly recall was a large black and white stray that found my father's and mother's farm a favorable place. My husband and I bought their place and moved in when they moved to a farm some ten or twelve miles away. That confused Old Tramp, and he traveled from place to place. There was no direct mail route between our homes, so we used Tramp for a mail carrier. When we wanted to send a message, all we had to do was to tie it around the dog's neck, and away he would go with a safe delivery. In a reasonable time we would find him with a reply or a note of incidents of the other place. Though there were no phones back then, our line of communication was never broken while we had Old Tramp to carry our messages.

Soon after we moved to the farm, my mother picked us up a small black puppy and came carrying it home in her arms on her horse. We named him Blacky, for his black fur really had a shine.

Blacky soon learned to hate hogs of every kind and color, especially as they roamed around in the road. His teeth must have been like needles, and his actions were as quick as lightning. He would tackle any hog, large or small, and send it haywire. Our neighbor did not like such treatment of their livestock, so one day when he took a dozen hogs squealing to their home, Blacky disappeared. The children sure took it hard. Some years later this neighbor told us he grew angry and shot little Blacky. I guess if there is such a thing as hog heaven, there were some happy hogs after this.

At Easter we always managed to give the youngsters in our neighborhood the pleasure of an Easter egg hunt. On this particular Easter, a rocky knoll at one of the neighbor's was selected. Blacky, the little dog, really enjoyed that hunt; so, also, did my son. He soon caught on that Blacky was smelling out the pockets of eggs and giving him the hint of where to look.

When we lost Blacky, nothing would do the children but to get another dog, so we found a real shepherd. His name was Rusty because of his color. He was well trained and would go over the fields and bring home the cows at milking time. He became my faithful companion and was never far away from me. I would take the children to gather wild strawberries, usually taking the baby too. I was foolish enough to lay the baby on a blanket and take it from place to place. Sometimes I would find myself quite a distance from my baby, but not Rusty — he was smarter than I, so he lay on the blanket for the boy's protection. An occasional snake crawled by and could have been dangerous, but not with Old Rusty near. We lost him with chlorea. He suffered, and so did I. At last I had to drip water into his mouth to quench his thirst. I shed tears for Old Rusty.

Good, faithful Old Rusty. I was in my late twenties then, and now I am in my nineties. It seems long, long ago. If dogs went to heaven, Rusty would be there. Yes, good old Rusty would be there.

We owned two more dogs during the years that we spent on the farm, Rover and Ted. I can't really recall the time or place when we obtained Rover, but he was a cute little puppy — another Shepherd with all the markings, and round as a butterball. We loved him from the first, but when he was about two months old, our farmhouse burned to the ground, and the puppy, Rover, was caught under the floor. Somehow he escaped, but we feared he would be blind as his eyes were red and glazed, but he recovered and proved to be a valuable addition to our farm. An old and dangerous barn stood on a hill a quarter of a mile from the house. How Rover, then five months old, sensed my fear that the old barn would fall and kill the twenty head of young cattle that fed beneath that roof is more than I can tell, but he proved that he could read my mind.

That old barn kept leaning from bad to worse. I complained, and at last my husband placed poles to lessen the danger. This did not allay my fears, so one day in the spring when the wind blew like a tornado, I went out in the yard and wondered if the barn could stand the strain. I thought if it could stand this, then I would not worry further. Just then it happened. I heard the squeak of breaking timbers, and, behold, the rotten old building slowly drew it last breath and lay in a heap. I took to my heels in a run for that hilltop, but puppy Rover out ran me, and when I got to the fence near the barn, there he was smelling and exploring over the fallen roof. To both our joy, there were no dead cattle. They were out on the hills looking for tidbits of spring grass. Rover met me, I'll say halfway with the good news. That's one time at least that I got a dog hug.

Poor Rover wasn't with us for too many years. Rusty must have left some of his germs, as Rover went the same Rusty did, with a burning fever.

Good old Ted. I might call him a jack of all trades. He could do almost everything but make a garden or hoe corn. He not only looked after our livestock on the farm, but also on my father's farm. My parents had moved back to an adjoining farm a half mile away from us, so Ted was available to both places. Neither farm had any substantial outside fences, for they were old and rotted away, but we didn't need fences as we owned old Ted. He knew each and every animal on both farms and kept them in their places. He went over the fields to inspect, but occasionally some stray animal would wander into my father's field. He would call me by phone and say, "Tell Ted his granddaddy needs him." I would go to the door and say, "Ted, your grandpa needs you." He knew exactly what I said, would raise up, lift one ear, and listen to hear my father's call from one-half mile away. Then off he took, but not to the house. He would go over the fields, and soon the stray animal was on its way. He usually came home without going to my father's house. Duty came before pleasure with Ted always.

As proof I will tell about the following incident. Our two boys had to go on an errand to town some twelve miles away. They went by horseback and let old Ted follow. Someone must have admired his handsome appearance and managed to shut him in. The boys had to come home without their dog. Of course, we all missed him and worried. We asked the merchant to make inquiries. I was looking out of my kitchen door, and there came old Ted, dear old Ted, in a long run. He didn't hesitate at the gate, but he made a beeline for the pasture fields in search of stray animals. I could hear his bark as he cleared the pasture. Then he came to the house, hungry and tired. He was met with many open arms in the family. It had been a long and watchful week for us all.

Now I will have to tell you about a small brown dog by the

name of Fuzzy. He first belonged to a neighbor, but somehow he got attached to Joe, my grandson, and decided to change residence or homes. The neighbors decided in time to give Fuzzy to Joe. My son-in-law was fond of the bottle, and when he came home from work he usually tried to slip his bottle along and secret it some place where my daughter, Faye, couldn't destroy it. Little Fuzzy somehow knew about the conflicting ideas and sided with Faye. One morning she was sweeping the living room, and she noticed the little dog performing queer antics. He lay down near a big chair, the cover of which reached the floor. He winked his eyes, twitched his ears, and sniffed under the chair. She could see that he was disappointed when she didn't move it. He went through a second act and more dramatics. At least, to please him, she decided to move the heavy chair and get his toy ball or mouse. To her surprise, it proved to be her husband's bottle. When she told him, he had a good laugh. He was a lover of dogs, especially of little Fuzzy.

Watch and Dane were two dogs which had a special love for their masters and seemed to always sense when they would be reaching home and by what route.

My brother's dog was named Watch, and he earned that title. He never missed sensing the way my brother, L. O., was traveling — as apt to come home by any one of the different roads that led to his place, but no matter which of them he took, there would be old Watch, three miles away from home, squatted on the side of the road, wagging his tail. Old Watch also looked after the children. One fall day my brother was helping a neighbor with the grain threshing not far from his home but across a deep brook. The two year old boy must have heard the noise of the machine and decided to help out. Anyway, his mother missed him after a time and frantically searched the premises. At last she started to walk to the thrashers for help and found old Watch holding on to the young lad to keep him from wading into the deep water. His clothes were torn to shreds. Poor Watch — he really had a tussle to prevent a drowning.

I know of a similar incident, as of that of old Watch, and it tends to prove to me that some dogs possess a second sense.

One of our friends moved with his family to a public place and could not take their small Scotch Terrier dog, so they did the next best thing and gave him to a nephew who would give him special care. The poor, lonely dog missed his master, who often made a special trip to see his pet. The dog, somehow, always knew when his old master was on his way. He sometimes took a round about road in order to shop in town. That road ended in an unused path through a long hollow, rough and strewn with rocks, but he was always met by the litle Scotch Terrier, squatted by the path and looking anxiously for his old master, who, in relating the story, did not understand how or on what route the dog knew he was taking. He must have had a hidden radar system.

    I think this will be my last dog story, which makes me wonder if animals fall in love. It seems this way in the case of my daughter's black and white terrier and the small yellow female of a nearby neighbor. They seemed to be life-long partners. The neighbor's dog's name was Curley. She was a small, yellow dog, who stayed with us as often as she stayed at home, next door. Things went along thus for several years, when someone was mean enough to place poison out for dogs. Little Curley was unlucky and got a dose of the deadly stuff. The mate was the first to call the attention of my daughter, by barking until she came to the door. When he made all the motions of asking her to follow, he led her to a small door that opened into the dark and dismal space under the floor. Then he almost pulled her to the dark recesses, where she found poor little Curley doubled up in deep pain. My daughter, Murrel, managed to get the small, suffering creature out into the light, but it was too late to do any good. Curley did manage to make it home and was placed in a small hall, where you could see her through a screen door. The family left her in her misery, but our dog stood by. By and by he came to beg Murrel to do something by taking her to the neighbor's, refusing any other route by pointing ahead and barking. Little Curley lay by the door dying, and our dog was left in deep distress.

Children's Tracks

Stuck out in the cement near the stacks I saw small barefoot children's tracks that skipped me back to so long ago, to write a time I am sure you do not know. To babes who sat upon my lap and where they often took their nap. I couldn't sing, but I could hum as we rocked in shade beneath the sun. Their tracks looked like the ones I saw, and my tear drops fell I will avow. No doubt all children's tracks are fear for those who hold them very near. The tracks in paint behind our door I thought I'd leave there ever more. But the house was burned down to the ground, and then the tracks were no more found. And there is the track in plaster white, it sticks and sticks with all its might. I would not erase it if I could — tracks leave memories that are good, and make a link with the long past. May be that is why they cling so fast. There were tracks of mud across my floor where small feet ran from door to door. And they showed mud between the toes, there was also soot upon the clothes, but all would fade out in the sud with elbow grease and enough of rub. There were many tracks out near the dam where little folks were catching clam. Those bare feet soon grew into shoes, such growth all mothers somehow rues. Too soon they lead off toward the school, and not much at home as a general rule. And then we wonder and ponder strong, can we direct the good and not the wrong? They grow so fast, these little tracks, that looked like those out by the stacks. Will they lead to paths of God and duty, or when all is done, will they be sooty?

This is the burden of mother's prayer
No matter whose small tracks or where,
For it breaks the heart if they return
All littered up with grime they learn.
And then we are filled with deep regret
And on and on till life's sun is set.
So, children dear, try to keep your tracks
Like small clean footprints out near the stacks.

Charley Chuckles

Mother and Father Chipmunk were as busy that fall day as little chipmunks usually are, hunting for nuts to carry to their den, when suddenly Mother Chipmunk called loudly, "Oh, Father, run — run for our lives. Farmer Brown is near with his gun, and little dog Bingo is on our trail."

Soon they found the pipe underneath Farmer Brown's old mill race. They followed along under cover, and little dog Bingo gave up the chase. Their hidden pipe led them into safety and also into a plentiful supply of food, stored away inside the tunnel where other little woods people had lived before. So Mother Chipmunk said to Father Chipmunk, "Here we shall spend our long winter months." They fed and fed and grew fat and lazy.

One cold day near Christmas time, Mother Chipmunk called to Father, "Oh, Father, come quickly. I have a little surprise for you." What a surprise! There in their cozy nest lay five new babies, oh so beautiful, except — except! Oh, what was that clucking noise that big boy chipmunk was making with his teeth. He gritted and growled and made Father so nervous. At last a pretty day came, and Mother decided to take her five babies out to the big stone into the sun. Father stretched and yawned, shook himself and decided he would venture out and see how his family was enjoying the beautiful sunshine. What a surprise he got when, for the first time, he saw Charley Chuckles. It had been dark in the tunnel. He said, "Oh, Mother, Mother, he is so big. Mother look at his eyes, look at his ears. They look like little dog Bingo's ears. Look at his color, he is black with white stripes." Mother said, "Oh, Father, maybe he will be all right. Wait and see. You know what a fright we got when Bingo chased us, and that owl that sat on the limb in the apple orchard. His eyes were as big and round as the moon. I was so scared. Then there was the striped skunk. You know how we ran for our lives."

But Mother could not comfort Father, so she took Charlie Chuckles back into the far corner of their tunnel and put him into the softest feather bed.

Father said, "Mother, tell me why Charley chuckles his teeth?" Mother said, "Oh, Father, he has two rows of teeth, and soon he will shed his baby teeth, and then he should no longer make that noise that makes you so nervous. I'll put Charley Chuckles to guard our tunnel so no little woods animals can disturb you, Father." So Father lay back and thought that was a good idea. He soon fell asleep.

Everything went well with the family of chipmunks hidden snugly in their dark tunnel. Sometimes Mother Chipmunk ventured out to check on the weather or to visit Farmer Brown's mill for special treats of food. One morning early in March Mother Chipmunk felt a special call to the wild woods. She peeped out the door, and the sun was shining bright, signs of good weather. Mother woke the four little chipmunks and made her way along with them to where Charley was guarding the entrance. She said, "I am taking the children for a hike into the big woods today. You see to Father Chipmunk and guard the door well," but out that door she went and what a hay day they had. They ate delicate shoots of green and, oh, the sweetest nuts.

But what about Charley? He hurriedly made up his mind. He had stood guard too long. He felt the call also of the great out of doors. So, Father or no Father Chipmunk, off he took. First he wanted to explore Farmer Brown's big mill. Mother had talked about this for so long. He climbed to the top of the big rock and took a look at the wide, wide world, where he expected to explore. Then, with one long leap, he reached Farmer Brown's mill. Mother hadn't told him of half the treasures Charley would now find out for himself. For the first time in his life he found enough grain to fill his empty stomach. He tasted of each and everything. By and by he felt he was growing sick. Oh, that awful pain in his stomach! He stretched himself out on the damp floor and must have passed out.

Soon Farmer Brown and little dog Bingo came and found Charley, seemingly dead. Farmer Brown had never seen an animal in all the woods that in any way looked like this one. He called little Bingo, but Bingo just shook his head. Farmer Brown felt for pulse and found a spark of life. He said, "Well, Bingo, we will see what's in the medicine chest." Here he found only castor oil, so he measured a few tablespoons of that and gave Charley. Then he found a big wooden box and put poor sick Charley inside it. When he thought it was secure, he sat and waited. Soon Charley gave out one of those hideous chuckles, made by his teeth.

Farmer Brown decided to take Charley, box and all, home with him and see what he could find out. He placed the door of the big owl cage over an opening in the box and punched and pounded until Charley was safe in the cage.

Then Farmer Brown called Mother Brown to come to see what he had found at the mill. They set the cage with Charley as a prisoner on the dresser. There Charley, for the first time, got a glimpse of himself in the big mirror. No wonder Mother Chipmunk had left him behind in the dark tunnel!

Farmer Brown decided that this strange animal surely must have escaped from some circus. There was a circus just being set up in a nearby town, so to that circus Charley must be taken. Farmer Brown walked the twenty miles to town, carrying Charley shut securely in his cage, and by his side little dog Bingo. The circus manager knew nothing about such an odd little animal, but after bargaining and arguments, Farmer Brown sold poor Charley

Chuckles to the circus manager. He would be put on exhibition.

But Charley had notions of his own. He had a glimpse of the big woods and a call to explore. He could dig his way out of the tight wire den that they had made for him. So when all was quiet Charley went to work. Now his chuckley teeth would aid his claws to dig his way to freedom. Before early dawn he had escaped from his secure pen, and now it was up to him to find his way through such traffic as he had never seen and find the big, big forest and woods people of his own kind.

Little did Charley Chuckles think of the difficulties ahead of him. He had searched from cave to cliff, from hill to hill all day long and found no one who resembled him or who could speak his language. Exhausted, he crawled under a cool cliff and fell asleep. He dreamed of Mother and Father Chipmunk and of the many little woods people he had met, but they all seemed to be scared of him.

He woke in the early morning, depressed, hungry and tired, but he didn't want to give up his dream or glimpse of freedom. The second day was worse and no more successful than the first. When Charley fell asleep he almost hoped he would die, but it was not to be that way.

When he awoke the sun was shining bright, the trees were full of leaves and, best of all, there were two little fairy creatures bending over him, asking where he came from, speaking his own language. He found himself telling them his life story (how strange). They told him of their wonderful wishing pond, where you could bathe and make a wish which always came true. Did Charley have a wish to make? He surely did: just to find himself to be a little striped chipmunk like his brothers and sisters.

So the good fairies took poor unhappy Charley Chuckles to their wishing Pond. When he had dipped himself into the sweet smelling water three times, he looked down into the clear blue water and saw, not his old self with big eyes like Mr. Owl, not with ears like little dog Bingo, not with stripes like the old skunk, he looked exactly like his little brothers and sisters in the tunnel.

Charley was happy for the first time. He sat up on his two hind feet and crossed his paws on his chest. He looked as though he was saying his prayers. Then he thanked the good fairies and took off into the big beautiful forest to find his own kin and people. He soon found himself a mate, so Charley Chuckles was happy ever after.

Legs For The Chiefty

By Betty Nutter Deitz

The little country school of Pine Grove stood far out in the country, surrounded by mountains and beautiful green trees. The boys and girls walked for miles to attend the school. During the noon hour the boys liked best to play "Fox and Hound," through the tangled woods. One day while playing, Ralph was the fox, chased by the hounds. To avoid capture, he broke through deep brush and made for the creek. What was his surprise when he stumbled onto a boy of his own age sitting among deep ferns, brush and wild violets, on the top of a cliff, looking much like he had grown into the scene.

Ralph forgot he was being chased by hounds. He soon found his new friend was named Tommy; that he had had an accident that left him unable to walk until his parents, who were poor, could earn money for an operation on his spine. He was happy to be carried to this shady spot among the trees, where he had made friends with so many small woods animals.

Ralph went to the nearby modest house and asked Tommy's parents if he and his schoolmates could come and carry Tommy to school for a visit. So Tommy became a frequent visitor to the small Pine Grove school. He was loved by everyone. At last he was named "Our Chiefty." His schoolmates began to wonder and plan how they could earn the money to pay for the legs of Our Chiefty. The opportunity came sooner than they expected. A nearby farmer had cut brush and cleared off a large tract of land for planting. There lay the big task of piling, clearing and burning. Tommy's schoolmates asked for the job. Soon the task was finished since the boys worked far into the night time. They had earned enough money to pay for their Chiefty's operation. How happy they were! More happy too were Tommy's parents, and how anxious for the result! How wonderful when the news came that Tommy would be able to walk. A few weeks passed by, and the pupils of Pine Grove were rushing out the door, anxious for their favorite game of Fox and Hound, when to their surprise, they saw a carriage stop and, what joy, to see their little Chiefty running to meet them, yelling, "I can walk!" They all yelled, "Legs for Chiefty, legs for Chiefty!"

Tommy was now one of the pupils of Pine Grove school. He could run through the woods and play Fox and Hounds with his schoolmates. He was so happy!

Poems

MY LAMB

Some one gave me a little lamb
At first I thought I'd name him Sam
But after all I named him Joe
But that was so long ago.

I built my lamb a little pen
He took the place and ran and ran
I told my friends, "That pen's for Joe."
But that was very long ago.

From out his pen Joe wanted much
I said to other, "Do not touch,
That pen belongs to my dear Joe."
But that was very long ago.

If out his pen he rushed
He'd take right off into the brush.
And then you'd hear me call, "Oh, Joe."
But that was very long ago.

He'd take to the woods with all its slush
Then I'd go off in such a rush.
My lamb would come when I'd call, "Joe."
But that was very long ago.

At last he grew out of his pen
Oh, what, Oh, what should I do then?
But I fenced a field in for my Joe
But that was very long ago.

Joe grew so fast and was such a pest
We had to tie him to the fence.
Oh, how sad I felt for my poor Joe.
But that was long, long ago.

When our lambs were sold to Mr. Biven
They thought my lamb should be given
But I said, "Oh on, oh no! Not my lamb Joe."
But that was very long ago.

Then my lamb turned out to be a ewe,
And many twins were born, I knew.
I still called her by name of Joe.
But that was very long ago.

I wouldn't attempt to count the kin
That from her stock derived have been
I still think of her as just my Joe
But that was very long ago.

This is the truth, some little lacken
For my memory does some hour slacken.
I did have a pet lamb, name of Joe
But that was very long ago.

That lamb of mine was white as snow
And followed me where e'er I'd go.
I was so fond of my lamb Joe
And that was very long ago.
     Betty Nutter Deitz

THE EARLY DAWN

It's bliss to match the mornings dawn
Its shadows creep across the lawn
To feel the freshness of the sweet breeze
To smell the fragrance of grass and trees.

The brook a trickling down the hill
The jingle of cow bells near the mill
The birds all flitting in and out
Small animals peeping all about.

As they venture forth from their deep lair
Calling to each other here and there
The new born flowers seemed full of glee
When tickled by feet of the early bee.

The old man in the moon seems pleased
As he looks from the sky on all of these
And the morning star shines oh! so bright
And dispels the darkness of the night.

Bright dew drops sparkle on grass and clover
Like a benediction through hills and over
Then the sun creeps up and sends its light
In hallowed streaks from dim to bright.

The cock sends forth his last loud call
Proclaiming day to each and all
The beauty of dawn has passed away
And comes the hurry of another day.

EARTH TO EARTH
AND DUST TO DUST

Earth to Earth and Dust to Dust
For the evil and for the Just.
For the aged and for the young
For those speaking in every tongue.

For all people of every race
From ages ago, we cannot trace.
"Earth to Earth and Dust to Dust"
For crowds of people on the street

For our loved ones we daily meet.
For those who live in far off lands.
And those who live on scattered strands.
For all who live, both you and me

For this is the way it has to be
"Earth to Earth and Dust to Dust"
For the cattle on a thousand hills
For the fish that play in brooks and rills.

For everything in depths of sea
For this is the way it has to be.
For all the shrubs and trees and flowers.
For the green grass and rosy bowers

"Earth to Earth and Dust to Dust"
But some day Gabriel will blow his horn,
And all will wake to a bright morn.
And call "Come forth, from sea to sea."

For this is the way it has to be
What a joy when all is well
No more sorrow from shore to shore
No more "Earth to Earth and Dust to Dust."

NO TIME

No time, no time to contemplate
No time, let's hurry or we'll be late
Life of late has been hurry, scurry
We had better rush and rush in a hurry

As time passes by we must rush much faster
No time, no time for fun and laughter
No time, no time to sit under our tree
Or to think and wonder how life should be.

We dare not falter or our pace relax
But labor and think of our income tax
We must work harder for there are the poor
That must be fed from out of our store

We must rush to town to see to our needs.
The desolate lawns and sow some seeds
Yes see to the needs of every day life
So filled with the hurry and scurry and strife

No matter what we come out in the hole
No time to count the course of this role
We must either sit down and give up the race
Or wear ourselves out in harness and trace

No time, no time, we must rush to the moon
Or the Russians will beat us there real soon
No time to explore in outer space
We must hurry, scurry into this race

We must hurry over to Vietnam
Or hurt the prestige of our Uncle Sam
We are in the race like a run away horse
And Uncle Sam is becoming more of our boss

As time goes on there will be more jobs
By people who think they are ruled by snobs.

MARCH 5TH, 1968

We thank you, God, for all things that count
Not just money of large amount
We thank you most for human kindness
For all there is of this old earth's mildness

We thank you for our children loyal
Who remember our days of sweat and toil
Thank you for things done for our relief
Through days of sorrow and of grief

Thank you for each day's bright hope
As through this life we slowly grope
Thank you for your willing pardon
Though we often wonder without regarding

Thank you for the small, small things
For sunshine and rain and the bird that sings
For the ills from which we are so spared
So many things we so much feared

Help us, Lord to be more grateful
To shun all things harsh and hateful.

DREAMS

A dream! a dream! the pesky thing
Where did it come from? What did it bring?
They trouble you in the midst of sleep
They call you back from the far away deep.

They come to you when they are not sought
They come to you and amount to naught.
If they are real nice, then you don't mind
But sometimes they seem so very unkind

And are all mixed-up with bugs and litter
That make you feel unclean and bitter.
But as I said, "If a dream is real nice
Then I wouldn't care if it came back twice."

I like the one where I flew over a mountain
And passed around twice over a deep blue fountain.
The hills all sparkled in a shimmery green
And shed an aura that I'd never seen.

The rocks all shone like silver and gold
And looked as perfect as if poured out of a mold.
The birds were flitting from tree to tree
And all was as pleasant as it could be.

I always liked dreams of flying around
Or of teaching children to fly above ground.
It's such a nice feathery feeling I get
And one can light down without even a net.

Then there are so many very good dreams
But one cannot figure out what they mean.
Then dreams I don't like are to be minus my clothes
I am more embarrassed than anyone knows,

Especially if teaching, and officials come in
I tell you! I'm as embarrassed as sin.
Or maybe worse is when in a crowd

And to lose my clothes is terrible, I've found.

Once in a while I've dreamed about snakes
I'll tell you now, it gives me the shakes.
Or to see a car go tumbling down hill
With someone I love is even worse still.

I dream quite often of friends who are dead
Sometimes it's real nice as I often have said
To walk together and talk as of old
So much like the past life again retold.

And so dreams go on, around and around.
Like the hands of a clock without any sound.
They say the mind never falters nor stops
But in dreamland it changes directions of hope

And picks up the threads of this and that
Much like the threads of a tangled old mat
That was woven of good and woven of litter
Much like our lives of good and bitter.

Here I sit writing on this Sabbath day
Because of the weather and inside I must stay
So here I keep writing about my dreams
For now there is nothing better it seems.

MY CANE

No, I couldn't do without my cane
I lean on it with might and main.
I grab for it when up at night
And hang right on with all my might.

Though it isn't very long in length
It adds to me a lot of strength.
So, I shall have to face the fact
I'll have to use a little tact

As I move around from place to place,
For in past years I've slowed my pace.
Not moving swift or strong or straight
Or feeling sure, secure or great.

I thought I'd never use a cane
But broken bones don't you sustain.
You may even think you are so strong
But after all you can be so wrong.

So, my good old cane is now my pet.
I'm glad that it and I have met.
It sits beside me by my chair
And stands nearby when in my lair

Doing ever what it can
Without complaint or a demand.
So my old cane will ever be
My staff, my shield for me, for me.

RICHWOOD TOWN

I see men pass with beaming faces
Fresh starting out on life's long race.
Though I see a future full of dread.
I see the one with cane in hand

Who has lived so long on this old land.
Life has been to him unkind
While he stumbles along toward a land divine.
It is not easy for him I know

To plod along so crippled and slow.
Now I watch some children as they play hop-toad.
Their hearts are glad, they carry no load.
They see not the shadow, that casts a cloud

O'er earth's horizen like a shroud.
Now I see a man with a crippled knee
By the side of a lad so full of glee.
Side by side they travel the road of life,

Sometimes so long and full of strife,
Sometimes as a mirror so bright and clear,
Sometimes in the depths of doubts and fear.
So goes life in this small friendly place
Where across the valley the mountains fall.

THE LAST LEAF

I am as lonely as lonely can be,
Hanging so high in my oak tree.
All my companions let loose today
And not a word did they have to say.

I watched as they flew way out over the tree
And I've sighed ever since as you can see.
Sometimes I hope a wind comes along
Then I will let loose and join my throng.

We could snuggle together near the old log fence.
We dreaded to go I'll have to confess
From this lone perch up in my tree
I've looked for a place I'd like to be.

But the cliff out yonder looks oh so cold,
I'd most as soon be under the mold.
Shall anyone miss me when I go away,
Though I was admired in my younger day.

I danced and sang the long summer through,
But now I have shed all my clothes so new.
I can dimly see away out, out there
A cloud that really doesn't look so fair.

I think its heading my way, I am now so sure
It's fierce I am afraid, I cannot endure.
Oh, I am caught in its cluthes so soon, so soon.
Now goodbye to the beams of the beautiful moon.

Goodbye to the leaves on my big bare tree.
Goodbye to the hum of the busy bee,
Goodbye to the birds and the children at play.
You have played in my shade since the first of May.

I am all dressed up for the cold winter blast,
I am settling down at last, at last,
And tumbling now and all in a flutter,
But I'm afraid it won't help to begin to mutter.

I am joining now my throng near the rock,
I hope to survive some of the shock.
My work is finished, and I've flown away.
I wish I could return the first of May,

Just when the violets come into bloom,
And I'd love again the big, bright moon.
I'd like to put on my pretty green gown
And wouldn't mind a shining bright crown.

But new leaves will come to take our place,
All shining and bright and edged in lace.
Now, goodbye, old earth, with all of your joys,
So many good things and all of your noise.

OUR OLD SUGAR CAMP

We loved our home on the slope of the hill
In twilight hours when all was still
We loved to see the sun peep out
And shed its luster all about.

Tall maple trees their shadows threw
Across the fields where daisies grew
But best of all was at the ramp
And round about the Sugar Camp.

We would take grain from the old mill
And scatter it around the hill.
The many birds would gather near
And seemed to have no thought of fear.

The squirrels would jump from tree to tree
As if to share in our glee.
But the best time was at the ramp
And round about the Sugar Camp.

In winter when snow was white
And the cold froze it then just right
We would take our sled and fairly flew
Over snow bank white and very new

And land at last at foot of ramp
And just above the Old Sugar Camp.
Old folks told their ghostly tales
And chills crept up our spine like snails

But we would love our sense of fear
When at the camp or very near
In the spring when the sap runs high
In our beds we love to lie

But we were tempted out to the ramp
To watch the workmen build the camp.
It was fun when the sparks would fly
And light our world from earth to sky

Soon issued from that lovely dell
The sweetest of the sweetest smell
That comes from the very best of sweets
That's made from cane or tree or beets.

Now that old camp has gone to decay
All trace of it rotted away.
Bushes and brambles cover the camp
And round about the Sugar Camp.

Now it is lonely as can be,
My tears are falling as you can see.
So is life with pain and losses
Mixed all along with joy and crosses.

OUR OLD OAK TREE

In memory I can plainly see
The image of our aged oak tree.
It stood on a knoll just out of our yard
Where people rested when they were tired.

It reached skyward so very tall
And spread swaying branches over all.
In spring time it turned the greenest green
And its leaves took on a waxen sheen.

But that old oak was so very tough
It had stood for centuries, its trunk was rough.
Why its bark was wrinkled we did not know,
While its leaves took on that extra glow.

Its limbs spread out across the branch
That trickled through our own small ranch.
And here is where we children played.
So many mud pies out there we made,

We gathered acorn lids for cups
And from the brook took long cool sups.
We carried moss from down the hill
And made our playhouses near the rill.

Sometimes playmates would come and be
With us out under our old oak tree.
There is where we had the best time
I think of it now as just sublime.

Often our dad would join in our fun
We would play hide and seek and run and run.
Under the tree we loved to play
Both early and late we were prone to stay.

In its shade was the grave of our little dog,
We made his monument from a small log.
His funeral was preached by my brother long,
But we all joined together in the song.

Then brother said we had better pray
And we wrote on the log, "The first of May."
We gathered violets and spread over his grave,
And then asked God his soul to save.

In that little brooklet that nearby ran
We tried so hard to build a dam.
But in spite of all it would spill over
And on down the hill spread over the clover.

But the awfulest thing happened, I would say,
It must have been near the middle of the day.
Some one said, "Oh, how very dark!"
Old Rover gave a howl and a long bark,

And what was that thing low in the sky?
Just a black, black cloud that was passing by.
A streak of lightning and a loud crack,
The ground seemed to heave and settle back.

We all ran and quickly jumped into beds
And just as quickly covered our heads.
When we ventured to look out the door,
Our old old tree stood there no more.

It was split apart and fairly shattered,
Above our yard we saw it scattered.
There never was such a sad, sad day.
From that time on, no place to play,

And all that was talked about for weeks
Was that awful storm and lightning streaks.
We were all heartbroken about our tree,
We could never play out there, our friends and we.

Spoofs

"Spoofing" was a favorite form of mountain entertainment, especially among the menfolk. They would trump up a situation, add a touch of creative larcency (all in fun, of course,) and perpertrate the act on an unsuspecting friend.

What follows are some examples of "spoofing" that I have been personally associated with, some of which are modern day spoofs. I hope you will enjoy these examples of tomfoolery, as my grandmother would have called it.

Dennis Deitz

Morel Madness

Morel mushrooms are a great delicacy, even more so than other edible mushrooms. For many years the best restaurants in New York City bought the wild morels from upstate New York, and (I have been told) saved them to serve to their best customers for thirty dollars an order.

Morel madness is a type of fever that hits certain people about the middle of April and lasts until about the middle of May, which is the season when morels appear. Modern medicine has not yet found a cure for this mania which lies dormant for eleven months.

Morels are a special type of mushrooms which do not look at all like most mushrooms, which resemble toadstools. The morels look more like sponges and are shaped like hayshocks sitting on little kegs.

Most city dwellers haven't even heard of morels unless they grew up in the country, but morel madness is not confined to West Virginia as people in many other states, especially northern states east of the Rockies, search for this elusive, delicious "vittle," and they also suffer from this same spring madness.

When I was growing up on the farm and going hunting I always liked to look for morels in the spring, and I still enjoy this. For me, hunting mushrooms has been a happy but frustrating experience. As an adult I hunted them some all through the years I worked, but not as I had when I was growing up or after I retired. When I was young we hunted them mostly in the open fields and under the apple and ash trees. They would be fairly good size and easy to spot because their dark brown color contrasted with the green grass. All through my working years I still looked for them in the same type of place, but when I returned and went morel hunting, most of them seemed to be found in the forests or deeper woods. These morels are smaller, harder to see and blend perfectly with the background. The leaves would be thicker over them, but I have more time to hunt now. I had just never hunted for them in the woods, and I had no old, open apple orchards to hunt in, so I had to hunt through the deep woods. I had to learn where they can be found now.

The most humilating part of this hunt comes from the reversal in roles from when I was a boy and now. I grew up as the country boy who knew every den tree within miles, the favorite feeding trees for squirrels, and every tree in the fields where morels could be found, and I watched the city slickers walk past the best places to find game, berries or morels without seeing them. Now I am the city slicker hunting morels in the woods and probably walking over or past them.

Finding the right areas, having the right weather conditions, getting the right sun angles, and knowing the certain trees the morels grow under are only the preliminary problems. No one who knows a good place ever shares with even his best friend where he finds morels, for if he does, the next spring when conditions are right he may find this favorite spot stripped clean of morels. So share his secret morel spots? Never!

In the area around Ansted and Hico in Fayette County, W. Va., there are stories of people gathering morels by the bags full. Finding where these spots are is the problem. One lady who did not know the unwritten rules asked a friend where she was finding so many morels, and the answer was, "Oh, the same place I found them last year."

People who get morel madness have certain unwritten codes of conduct: they never advertise this madness to their urban friends as they don't want any of them to get morel madness, for competition is neither wanted nor is desirable — morels are too scarce and hard to find. They never tell anyone where their favorite places are to look, and they develop a mythomania about where and how many morels have been found. After all, this delicacy is only an edible, umbrella-shaped fungus, which is often found growing wild in pastures, lawns or golf courses where the grass is kept short, and the ground is enriched by manure, especially horse manure. Who would want to eat such things? Eat fungus? Heavens to Betsy, Yes!

Our daily newspaper carried an article by Adrian Gwin about how morels were being found in Kanawha Forest, with some people getting a large bag full. I got fired up with morel fever and was ready to go hunting for them, but conditions never got exactly right: there must be rain followed by a warm night. I went anyway. I climbed high hills. I checked under poplar trees which were easy to spot as they are among the first trees to "green up" in the spring. I walked miles and found a few. Were they hard to see! They were only as large as hickory nuts and blended perfectly with the dead brown leaves, mostly pushing up underneath the leaves, out of sight. I came home with my large bag not really having been needed as I could carry my morning's gathering in the palm of my hand,

and I hadn't even used half a tank of gas in my travels.

I don't think my wife ever did understand when I explained that this was one of the ways early man had provided for his family.

I got acquainted with the Park Superintendent at Kanawha Forest, and I was sure I had it made, for he did give me some good advice: search the top part of the coves facing south and, of course, after a warm rain.

I am sure he showed me where he saw people coming out of the woods with the grocery bags full. I am equally sure that he was like all morel hunters; he kept secret his favorite, private little spots where he found morels. I am also sure if he had been asked about these private places he would have answered, as would have all members of the morel hunters society, "The same place I found them last year."

After getting the Park Superintendent's advice I did better, for I found a bigger handful. I brought them home, and my wife fried them in butter. What a great tasting appetizer! I was eager for the next warm rain, which never came until the season was over. Of course, those few were enough to give me some bragging rights, and as I told and retold about finding them, the amount I had found continued to grow with each telling. I quit describing them from a handful and used numbers as the morels were very small, and numbers sounded more impressive. Also, I was always good in mathematics and could easily add to the numbers.

After five years I still have the same wrinkled grocery bag waiting to be filled.

One spring a young couple moved close to us, and they loved to hunt morels and walk in the woods too. Also, Tom said he knew the place to go in Lincoln County. He said he had a working buddy who had filled a grocery bag, so, on his next day off, Tom, his wife and I took off to find that spot. Even though we had not had a warm rain for four or five days, we found a couple of handfuls, so maybe his friend had broken the code of morel hunters and had told us more than, "Where I found them last year."

When I got home with my handful of morels, I could hardly get my right knee bent enough to get out of the car, for I had twisted it. For the next two months I had to go up steps by stepping up with my left foot, then dragging my right leg up to the step, and then repeating on the next step. My wife never did understand my handful of morels was worth a tank of gas and two months of dragging my right leg along, but wives don't always understand perfectly logical things, like this.

Last spring I stopped in a book store in Oak Hill, and the owner of the store was a lady who was chomping at the bit with morel fever. The morel hunters were out in droves, and, as she had to keep her store open, she felt chained up. Even though she had gained a lot of weight during the winter and her blood pressure was sky high, she just had to follow the trail of the morels. She was trying to find someone to keep the store open for her. She was true to the morel hunter's code: where she always found them was a vaguely described mountain which couldn't be found starting from Oak Hill. You had to start from another vague point which couldn't be explained, but it was exactly where she had found them last year. She did offer some good advice: always look under the poplars or walnut trees where the cove faces the morning sun. Always hunt uphill as you can see where the winter leaves have been pushed up by the growing morels, for you have a better angle to see this evidence. Then, when you find a few, always look in line with the ones you find as prevailing winds will scatter the seed or spores in some certain direction. Could I fail if I followed this good advice? Never. I had the fever, so I found a likely looking spot and went hunting. I didn't find any morels, but I probably had the distinction of being the only morel hunter in that entire country who was out hunting in a suit with a white shirt and tie.

Now I feel I am really ready for a great year for harvesting morels, for a girl working in a gift shop told me exactly where she and her husband found two grocery bags full in a couple of hours. I am to go exactly two and a quarter miles out the Springtown Road to a white farm house and ask the people for permission to hunt morels. They will be glad to let me go if I share with them. In my saner moments I know that the house is not on the Springtown Road, but on the Sunday Road, and it will be 4½ miles, not 2-1/4 miles. Naturally these names I am giving are not the right names of the road and not the same distance out, and I am certain in my normal moments I will find them and will be able to join that group of morel hunters who, when asked, will say, "I found them the same place I found them last year." This will fullfill a great ambition I have.

I have figured out some ways to recognize morel madness in people, and I am listing them below:

1. When someone you haven't believed for eleven months tells you where to look, and you believe everything the person says,

2. When someone whose word you have utterly trusted for eleven months starts torturing and twisting the truth beyond recognition about where to find morels,

3. When someone believes every "No Trespassing" sign is just a cover-up for bags of morels,

4. When you eagerly seek the advice of someone you haven't spoken to for eleven months because of the way he had mis-guided you the year before,

5. When a young husband deserts his pregnant wife who is

ready to go to the hospital to deliver at any moment to go to his favorite moral hunting ground and finds his wife there ahead of him (morel hunting affects both men and woman),

(It has occurred to me to wonder if this wife had given birth to a boy in the "morel patch," would they have named him Morel Mushroom? If the baby had been a girl would they have named her Molly Moocher, the regional name for morels? If the family surname were Mollohan or McClanahan, either name would have a nice ring to it, wouldn't it?)

(Where did the colloquialism Molly Moocher originate? I can only guess that a lady named Molly had the habit of mooching morels on the neighbor's mountain or in the meadow.)

6. When a young man's fancy turns from love to morel hunting, THEN, without looking at the calendar, you know it's April.

When April showers bring forth May flowers, morel hunters are also brought forth.

Mountaineer Mania, Or What About Them 'Eers?

I-79, or the road to Morgantown.

There are a lot of theories and even books written about how John F. Kennedy came into West Virginia in 1960 and won a presidential election. JFK was a Catholic and went head to head with his opponents and the people in a very protestant state. The analysts first said this was impossible — for him to win West Virginia. After the election many theories were advanced as to how he attained the one-sided victory: money, how he used the anti-Catholic vote to an actual advantage; how he used youth, good looks and charm to win.

Personally, I don't agree with any of these theories. The election was held in the fall, during football season, or when Mountaineer Mania had afflicted almost the whole state. This was at a time when the road to Morgantown was a long six to eight hour, torturous trip from the southern part of the state.

My theory is that JFK's political team began to let the word get around that there would be a new four lane road to Morgantown if JFK were elected. It is no wonder that he won the southern part of the state by a landslide when the Mountaineer Mania was at its highest pitch! This promise was kept, and the road to Morgantown is now I-79.

Through the years many football and basketball players were carriers of a disease called "Mountaineer Mania." They were the "Typhoid Marys" of West Virginia sport fans. The early ones I remember reading about were mostly football players. One of the earlier disease carriers was Ira (Rat) Rodgers, an all American fullback. The early twenties had many football players who were carriers of this disease under a great coach, Clarence "Doc" Spears. Later I knew two or three of these carriers of Mountaineer Mania. The one I knew best was Nate Rohrbaugh, a great basketball coach at Glenville College while I was there as a student. He coached all sports at Glenville College. He had played both football and basketball at WVU in the early twenties, and for the next thirty years was considered an all-time, all-West Virginia guard in both basketball and football.

In the early 1930's I saw Joe Stydahar, a 6'4" center, play his first game for WVU in basketball. He was almost a freak playing basketball at this unbelievable height, but today he couldn't play anything but guard at that height.

Stydahar was a carrier of "Mountaineer Mania" as a football player. He, Harry Clark and Bill Karr were later all-pro football players with the "Monsters of the Midway," the Chicago Bears.

In the early thirties, the WV boxing teams were the leading carriers of the fever, far out-ranking the basketball teams and even the football players. They always ranked in the top five teams in the nation.

As a member of the Glenville boxing team I was matched with "Pete" Puglia, a boxer who never lost a bout in his career. I had never been inside a ring before, and maybe had not seen a ring before. If meeting someone better than you are is a great way to improve, I surely should have been improved a lot that night.

In the late 1930's some of the carriers of the Mountaineer Mania were Harry Lothes and "Squint" Phares from Elkins. Later Harry Lothes was a good friend of mine at Union Carbide. Many people spoke of seeking Harry, an old set-shot artist, shooting his high set-shots, with the basketball disappearing into the darkness of the rafters in the old Mountaineer field house, and then knocking the bottom out of the basket.

The first basketball team that became real carriers of Mountaineer Mania was the 1942-43 team. That team won the NIT tournament, which was equal to winning the NCAA today. WVU was the last team invited and was called the Cinderella team of the tournament. Only one player was more than six feet tall.

For the next twenty years this Mania spread like a blanket over the state. Their winning record was second in the nation for a twenty-five year period. The number of players who played to infect the state is too numerous to list. The All-American players started with Leland Byrd, then Fred Schaus (later the coach), Mark Workman, Hot Rod Hundley, Rod Thorn, and the greatest of them all, Jerry West, who was a great all-pro with the Los Angeles Lakers.

Harry Lothes, a basketball player in the late 1930's and a WVU basketball coach for a short time, came to work for Union Carbide in the personnel department, and one of his duties was running the plant league sports. Since I played sports, with the help of Harry I formed a little league in baseball, and I knew him well for many years, until his untimely death. We swapped stories.

He told about attending a coal league baseball game near

Morgantown. One team had a big, strong looking player who came to bat and was hit in the head by a wild pitch. This was before protective helmets were used. The ball went off the batter's head, straight up in the air about twenty-five feet. The batter just stood at the plate, his bat still cocked to hit, never looking away from the pitcher. The foul ball dropped back into the catcher's mitt, and he returned the ball to the pitcher. The pitcher picked up the resin bag, rubbed up the resin. The batter still stood at the plate, perfectly still, bat still cocked. The crowd buzzed. Fans were telling each other that the batter was the toughest person they had ever seen. About the time the pitcher finally got ready to pitch, suddenly the batter fell flat on his face. He was in the hospital for about two weeks.

Another time Harry told me about the time he was trying to get a little sympathy and understanding from Oscar Fudge.

Among Harry's duties in personnel work was making rulings in the intramural sports. Sometimes a team might enter a protest against another team, wanting a forfeit of a game for maybe using an ineligible player. Many times the case was judgment rather than being covered with a clearcut ruling. Harry hated these cases because he didn't care for controversy as he liked everyone.

One day, after having to make a decision in a no-win situation, he happened to meet Oscar Fudge and started telling him his troubles. He told Oscar, "You know that you are an S.O.B. if you do and you are an S.O.B. if you don't."

Oscar, in his deep South Carolina accent, told Harry, "Y'all know that you remind me of a town judge back in C'alina. A black man was in 'cout' for cuttin' another black man's face all over during a knife fight. The jedge, knowing everyone in town by their first name, started to chewing the black man out. He said, 'John, how could you cut a man's face like that and disfigure his face for life? etc., etc.' Finally, John was able to ask, 'But, Mr. Judge, what would you do if somebody called you a black S.O.B.?' The judge up and said, 'John, you are being ridiculous. No one is a black S.O.B. I'm not even black.' John then said, 'Mr. Judge, then what would you do? Just suppose they was to call you whatever kind of S.O.B. you is.?' "

Harry laughed and advised me to never go to Oscar Fudge for sympathy.

Art "Pappy" Lewis

"Pappy" Lewis was the WVU football coach of the football glory years of the 1950's. His greatest asset to WVU was as a recruiter. His first year as coach he recruited more good West Virginia players than had been recruited for years. No hill was too high nor a valley too deep for "Pappy" to look for football players. He found the great Sam Huff in a coal camp. He got Bruce Bosley from the hills of Pocahontas County, Bob Orders and Bobby Moss came from Huntington, Tammy Alman from Charleston, and on and on in the by-ways and backwoods.

My favorite story of "Pappy" Lewis's recruiting was the time he went looking for a high school boy living up a deep, long hollow. He followed the narrow paved road for a few miles and then went on a dirt road to the end. After walking a path, he came to the home of this great prospect, a small mountain cabin, but there was no one at home. Instead, there was a sign on the door: Gone to the country.

"Pappy" Lewis's success as a recruiter lay in his ability to be almost a part of the family, anywhere from a shack to a mansion. I can imagine "Pappy" being at home in the shacks and cabins as he had grown up a poor boy, living just across the Ohio River from West Virginia. I can picture him sitting at the kitchen table with the football player's mother, maybe sharing the bitter black coffee, or even the juice of the corn, the brown beans and cornbread, the leather britches beans, possum, sweet potatoes, sassafras tea, and maybe even ramps. Also any variety of ethnic foods.

He complimented the mother and enjoyed the food and drinks in exact proportion to the strength, the size, and the athletic ability of her football-playing son.

I have more trouble picturing "Pappy" recruiting in a mansion. I just can't picture this great hulk of a man perched on the edge of a fragile chair, drinking weak tea from an equally fragile cup, nibbling on a tiny hors d'oeuvre, almost hidden by a huge thumb and forefingers. Just picture the other ham-like hand trying to hold the cup in a dainty manner with his little finger waving at a 90 degree angle from the others, trying manfully to denote genteelness and parlor manners. At any rate, he was successful in both cases.

I have always had a theory that "Pappy" Lewis's most effective argument to the Mountaineer papas was that a college education would greatly aid the son's ability with a still.

Mountaineer Mania lives on into the 1980's, as evidenced by the recent flashing lights on the top of a Charleston bank: Beat Pitt.

Fred Schaus

I first met Fred Schaus when he was a basketball player at WVU. His college roommate was the son of a friend of mine and worked with my brother. We used to make the long journey to Morgantown to see the basketball team play. We would stop at their room with Mr. Satterfield. Fred Schaus was then an all-American player known as "Fireball Freddy."

After playing several years as a professional basketball player, Fred Schaus returned to WVU as the basketball coach through the "glory years" of WVU basketball, coaching such All-Americans as the great Jerry West and Hot Rod Hundley. Mr. Schaus is now the athletic director.

Coach Schaus has been in our home as the last player he ever recruited at WVU was our son, Jaye. About two weeks later, he resigned as basketball coach. I have never been able to figure out whether there was any connection between the two events.

How To Recognize Mountaineer Mania

When your mania rises and ebbs with each win and loss.

When you want to help build a monument to the coach after each win and are willing to help hang him in effigy after each loss.

When you want the Mountaineer football coach fired because he didn't try to recruit your favorite high school halfback, weighing 140 pounds, and you just know that he would have made the greatest power-running fullback the Mountaineers ever had. Or maybe your favorite high school lineman at 175 pounds would have made a one-man line all by himself if the coach hadn't been too dumb to recruit him.

When every year for fifty years you believe the annual buildup by the publicity department and the sports writers. That is, every year you are convinced that this is the year, regardless of how logic tells you what the outlook actually will be.

When you can sit in the stands and can't believe what a dumb play the coaching staff has just called. Or when you can watch TV and still recognize these dumb calls or even recognize these dumb calls by listening on radio.

A dumb call by the coaching staff is easy to recognize by anyone afflicted by Mountaineer Mania. It is any play called which doesn't work. Any fan afflicted by Mountaineer Mania immediately knows that this was a dumb call. Any time a play is called that doesn't work was never the right call. All of us afflicted knew what would have worked. Any play other than the one called.

Another thing all of us, "the afflicted," know so much more about than the coaches is the quarterback positions. Even though we have been shouting from the hilltops and the valleys about having the greatest quarterback in the nation, we immediately know better if he makes a mistake, such as throwing an interception. We always know that he shouldn't have been playing in the first place. We all know that even the third-stringer was a much better player at quarterbacking.

You would think that WVU would have a great coaching advantage over almost any school in the country. What other school has the help of the whole state in giving advice about recruiting, play-calling, who should have made great players, and coaching?

It is as though the coaches think that all of this "free" advice is worth just what they pay for it.

The Carbide Retirees Bridge Club

By Dennis Deitz

Since retiring I have joined the Carbide Retirees Bridge Club, which had been organized about the time I retired. Although I have played bridge for many years, it was mostly with one of my brothers and a couple we both knew. Since my brother's death fifteen years ago, I hadn't played one hand of bridge since. Did that stop me? Never!

When I started playing bridge with this group, I began to hear of the great bridge masters, Goren, Sheinwald, Blackwood, etc. Did I let this influence me? Not in the least! I had my own system that I had used all of my life in everything. It had gotten me places, though not places many people would like to be. Through all of this I have been consistent in using my own personal system, which I call the KISS system, i.e., KEEP IT SIMPLE STUPID. This may be bad bridge but it's a good philosophy.

Just because many in the group had played all their lives and had taken lessons from experts, knew many of the systems of bidding to signify their card holdings, and had gotten to be good players, I wasn't intimidated in the least. I over bid by about two in any system used. I still think I'm right. I make some real high scores, but mostly for the opponents. My philosophy was that I had gone to play cards with no points and any points I made was a net gain. I always have to have a philosophy about everything, figuring that even a poor philosophy is better than no philosophy at all.

The Carbide Bridge Club was thus a mixed group, all using their own individual expert systems. Also, there were visitors or those who would play a few times during the year, plus new retirees. This led to a lot of interesting bidding. A cue bid from one system would be answered by a response from the partner's pet system, resulting in some great final bids. The ringing shout of "dummy" was not necessarily criticism or a reflection on playing ability, but the need for a bidder at a three-person table.

Now we had our system of changing partners and tables after

each round of four hands, which went something like this: The tables were numbered one through six, depending on the number of players we had for the afternoon. We drew numbers in color. Say a player started out at Table 3. Everytime he won he moved to a lower number until he reached Table 1. There he stayed until he lost. Table 1 was the "Top of the Hill" table. Only the losers would move to the highest numbered table or No. 6 in this case.

This led to some hilarious confusion at times. This system worked out very well as long as our leader, Eston Swartz, was there. He could keep us all fairly well straightened out. One Tuesday Eston was absent. Confusion reigned. One of our more articulate members took over. He could make a speech at the drop of a hat and was willing to drop the hat. He got up and gave us a very logical speech of instructions . . . very convincing.

The only problem was that the winners were suddenly moving in the opposite direction or to a higher numbered table. The losers thought that they were told to move to a lower numbered table. This worked fine during the first round. Then we changed tables. The winners moved up and the losers moved down. We had eight people at every other table and none at the in-between tables. Then we would receive another lecture about being unable to count from one to six. Every one understood exactly until it came time to change tables again when confusion would reign, requiring another lecture in mathematics, especially on the numbers one through six. One of the ladies timidly suggested that we go to the more familiar system of counting 6-5-4-3-2-1. She was scorned as a traitor to "hillbilly ciphering." The mathematic ability of our parents was also questioned. How had they ever figured out how to get together to multiply? After another thorough lecture, everyone understood the new rules where the winner would move to a higher number and the loser stay at the table. The only problem was that the next week the fill-in-leader had forgotten what his system was for the week before.

In our bridge group we have a number of people who had spent a career in higher mathematics, and I just know that they were enjoying the confusion and speechifying more than they were the bridge game.

We also have what we call our "After" experts. After the bidding is over and the hand is played, they will share their expertise on how the bidding should have been handled and the hands played, quoting all of the Masters. In spite of our plea for help *before* the hand is played, would they help? Never, just AFTER. Does this help? Not at all. The hand is just over and gone forever and our opponents just refused to let us play it over correctly, with Goren or Blackwood at our shoulder.

Our quite capable leader, Eston Swartz and his wife, Doris —

also a member of our bridge group — have returned to their birth places in Illinois. However, Nate Clauss is taking over for Eston. Nate is an intelligent, precise engineering type with almost a half century experience and training in having every line exact and correct. How will he handle us who are never exact and seldom correct? Will it blow his mind when he sees eight of us trying to get in four chairs at one table while the four chairs at the next table remain empty?

Will we still mill around aimlessly? Will the final plaintive words be, "Where am I supposed to go now?" We can only wonder what the future holds.

Archie And The Diesel Cadillac

Archie, a friend of mine, owned a diesel Cadillac a couple of years ago. A while back, he and his wife went to Connecticut to visit a daughter. While driving around, the diesel engine began giving out great clouds of black smoke. He took the car to Cadillac garages. They had no idea what was wrong, had no idea when they could work on it. Archie decided to start home anyway, with great clouds of black smoke in his wake.

Then came the toll gates. The first one he came to, a woman toll gate keeper came choking and gasping out of the booth, yelling, "Get that thing out of here! Get it out! You are going to blow up all of the booths!" When he came to other booths and service stations, he starting coasting into the last one-half miles, thus eliminating the black smoke behind him. Then he would take off again, leaving the booths and highways completely hidden in a great, black cloud. No traffic passed him as the drivers couldn't even see the road.

Still the smoke-making diesel Cadillac rolled south past Philadelphia to Route 48, turning west into the teeth of the prevailing winds. Then the Weather Bureau began to get excited. They began excitedly calling each other about a phenomena they had never seen before. They reported that a great, dark, black cloud was rolling over the hills and through the valleys west, opposite to the way the winds were blowing.

Then the CB'ers began to warn each other to take detours onto other roads, if possible. If not, to pull over and roll up the windows.

Finally, Archie smoked his way into Morgantown, West Virginia, home of WVU, for the night.

The excitement wasn't over. By the next day after Archie left Morgantown, the scientists at WVU were making excited calls to other researchers, both over the air and by telephone. They had spent years trying to convert coal into gas. Now they were reporting that some hillbilly coal miner had found how to burn coal directly into his diesel engine.

When the environmentalists heard this news over the air, they got into the act. They called their lawyers. They called their Congressmen. They called each other to organize a campaign to stop the use of coal being used to fuel cars directly.

Finally, Archie arrived at home, leaving the scientific world and the public mystified. He also left central West Virginia with a black cloud extending from Morgantown to Charleston.